"Wendy Behary has dedicated decades to understanding narcissism, both as a clinician and a scholar. In *Disarming the Narcissist*, she distills these hardwon insights into a very readable form. This book is a terrific resource for those looking to better understand narcissism."

> —**W. Keith Campbell, PhD**, professor in the
> department of psychology at the University of
> Georgia and author of *The Narcissism Epidemic*

Praise for the first edition

"Anyone whose life predicament includes dealing with a narcissist will be well-advised to read Wendy Behary's book and heed her advice. *Disarming the Narcissist* offers sound suggestions and keen insights—a breakthrough in one of psychology's toughest cases."

> —**Daniel Goleman**, author of *Emotional Intelligence*

"This is a timely and important book. Behary offers a uniquely well-articulated exploration of the complexities of living with a narcissist, conveyed in a clear and elegant writing style. *Disarming the Narcissist* provides a treasure of insightful observations and strategies to help those working or living with a narcissist. Behary's wisdom and warm humanity, together with her wide understanding and successful integration of interpersonal neurobiology and schema therapy, provides a fresh perspective that will help the reader make sense of relationships that often seem so confusing and give them tools to do something about it. I recommend this book heartily."

> —**Marion F. Solomon, PhD**, author of *Narcissism and
> Intimacy* and *Lean on Me*

"...a valuable contribution to the growing self-help literature on the fascinating subject of narcissism. Behary takes the reader step-by-step through a process of understanding our personal triggers to the wounding inherent in narcissistic relations and then lays out a pathway for personal empowerment and change."

> —**Sandy Hotchkiss, LCSW**, author of *Why Is It Always About You?*

"For the practicing clinician there is perhaps no other group of clients more difficult to work with or that generates more fear and feelings of inadequacy than narcissists. In *Disarming the Narcissist*, Behary has provided both the theoretical knowledge and practical advice necessary for clinicians to understand, empathize and, thus, help this challenging group of clients and their partners. Her 'disarmingly' straightforward, accessible style and impressive clinical experience make this a very valuable book indeed."

> —**William M. Zangwill, PhD**, director of EMDR Associates

"Behary is an exceptionally perceptive, compassionate, and creative clinician and an outstanding teacher. I have always found her immersed at the cutting edge of clinical science and practice. It has been both a privilege and an inspiration to watch her vision and clinical contributions evolve. These remarkable qualities are clearly evident in her new book, which I have no doubt will make a major contribution. It will bring anyone who deals with narcissism fully up to date with the latest our field has to offer, articulated in clear, poignant, and practical terms."

> —**George Lockwood, PhD**, director of the Schema Therapy Institute Midwest in Kalamazoo, MI

disarming
the
narcissist
SECOND EDITION

Surviving & Thriving
with the Self-Absorbed

WENDY T. BEHARY, LCSW

New Harbinger Publications, Inc.

Publisher's Note

Distributed in Canada by Raincoast Books

Eighteen Early Maladaptive Schemas © 2003 Jeffrey Young, PhD. Unauthorized reproduction without the written consent of the author is prohibited.

Copyright © 2013 by Wendy Behary
New Harbinger Publications, Inc.
5674 Shattuck Avenue
Oakland, CA 94609
www.newharbinger.com

Cover design by Amy Shoup; Text design by Michele Waters-Kermes; Acquired by Tesilya Hanauer; Edited by Jasmine Star

Library of Congress Cataloging in Publication Data

Behary, Wendy T.
  Disarming the narcissist : surviving and thriving with the self-absorbed / Wendy T. Behary, LCSW. -- Second edition.
      pages cm
  Includes bibliographical references.
  ISBN 978-1-60882-760-2 (pbk. : alk. paper) -- ISBN 978-1-60882-761-9 (pdf e-book) -- ISBN 978-1-60882-762-6 (epub) 1. Narcissism. 2. Interpersonal relations. I. Title.
  BF575.N35B44 2013
  158.2--dc23

                                        2013014290

Printed in the United States of America

22   21   20

20   19   18   17   16   15   14

This book is dedicated to the memory of my "Poppy," Norbert V. Terrie—a true knight, a loving and generous man, my father.

Contents

Foreword

Over the years, one of the most common issues that my clients have brought into therapy is how to deal with the self-centered, egotistical behavior of narcissistic partners. These clients almost always feel frustrated, angry, demeaned, and helpless over the almost total lack of sensitivity and empathy their partners show for their needs and feelings. I myself often sit in sessions in disbelief as I hear story after story describing the degree of selfishness these clients have to put up with. So often my clients can't seem to find the strength to either leave or stand up to the narcissists they fell in love with years ago.

I am so excited that my close friend and colleague Wendy Behary has written this definitive book on dealing with narcissists to help the countless number of people who, like my clients, try to live or work with narcissists on a daily basis. While there are several other self-help books on this topic, *Disarming the Narcissist* addresses the issue with great sophistication, depth, and compassion and offers highly effective strategies for change. Wendy has devoted years of clinical practice to the specialized treatment of narcissists and their partners, making her the perfect author to tackle this very difficult and resistant problem.

Wendy draws on two fields of science and therapy to help the reader better understand and deal with narcissism: schema therapy and interpersonal neurobiology. Schema therapy is an approach I and my colleagues have been developing over the past twenty years to help therapists, clients, and others better understand the deep emotional themes, or schemas, that begin when we are children and eventually lead most of us to engage in repetitive and self-destructive life patterns. I first presented these ideas for the general reader in *Reinventing Your Life*.

Disarming the Narcissist extends the concepts of schema therapy into work with narcissism and includes fresh insights and perspectives that I had never envisioned before reading this book. Wendy provides a wonderful explanation of how schemas like defectiveness and emotional deprivation affect our lives in dramatic ways. Her unique contributions to schema therapy lead us to a deeper understanding of the narcissists in our lives, as well as showing us how to overcome our own "demons" that keep us from dealing effectively with narcissistic partners, parents, friends, and colleagues.

I am pleased that Wendy has gone so far beyond the clichés and simplistic advice that many other books and therapists offer. There are no simple answers or techniques when it comes to changing narcissism. You will have to delve into this book and work hard to truly understand the wealth of material presented here, but the rewards will be commensurate with your effort. You will learn about the different categories of narcissists, the range of strategies that narcissists so skillfully employ to disarm you and even convince you that you are to blame for their complaints, and the importance of empathic confrontation as a method of communicating with and standing up to narcissists. Wendy offers invaluable suggestions on ways to develop and sustain compassion for narcissists, even when you are being mistreated, and on how to create enough leverage to convince a narcissist to change. *Disarming the Narcissist* also provides rich case examples that bring this approach to life.

If you put in the time required to understand the insights Wendy describes and practice the techniques she offers, you will, probably for the first time, have a set of tools that shift the odds in your favor in your relationship. You will have a newfound confidence that you know how to respond when your partner humiliates you in front of friends and family members or says things like

"You're so stupid if you can't see that my way is the only intelligent one."

I want to conclude by emphasizing a point that Wendy makes repeatedly in this book—a point that is central to schema therapy. As with any other personality problem, we need to approach narcissists and those who live with them in a compassionate way. Most narcissists are not "evil" or "bad" at a deeper level, no matter how they treat us. If you can learn to assert your rights while simultaneously working hard to reach the vulnerable, lonely core of the narcissist in your life, you stand a much better chance of bringing out the side of your partner that can love and care for you.

I know of no better way to achieve this compassionate road to change than to start reading *Disarming the Narcissist* now. As Wendy says in her conclusion, "The self-help journey can be both lonely and arduous." But the dramatic changes in your relationship will usually more than repay your efforts.

I recommend this outstanding book to anyone who lives with, works with, or treats narcissists—including their partners, work associates, family members, and therapists.

—Jeffrey Young, PhD

Director, Cognitive Therapy Center & Schema Therapy Institute of New York

Faculty Member, Department of Psychiatry, Columbia University Founder, International Society for Schema Therapy

Preface

I f you are in a relationship with someone who exhibits the traits of a narcissistic individual, don't think twice before you enter this book. In *Disarming the Narcissist*, Wendy Behary offers a practical tool kit that gives us insights into how we can manage the emotional challenges of relating to someone who does not relate to us: the narcissistic individual.

This gem of a how-to survival guide is filled with useful tips informed by two branches of science: the cognitive science view of how the mind is organized around schemas and my own field—interpersonal neurobiology. Schemas are generalized filters that bias our perceptions and alter our thinking. For two decades, the author has immersed herself in schema therapy and treatment of those with narcissism as their major issue in psychotherapy. Using this science background and her practical experience as a therapist, Wendy Behary walks us through easy-to-understand explanations of how the mind of a narcissist works. We come to see the schemas that organize how a narcissist sees the world, and how that perspective is often devoid of interest in the internal world of others.

Interpersonal neurobiology examines the connections among relationships, the mind, and the brain. Our professor of how-to-get-along-with-a-narcissist, Wendy Behary, has been studying this field intensively with me for many years, and she has deftly applied it to her own area of expertise in dealing with these individuals who lack the knack of empathy. The circuits in the brain that enable us to imagine the internal subjective experience—the mind—of another person may not be well developed or easily accessed in the narcissist. *Mindsight* is our capacity to see the mind itself, in ourselves and in others, and in narcissists it is often poorly developed. Therefore, relationships with such an individual will feel lopsided: conversations and interactions are all about the other person, not about you or the two of you as a "we."

This lack of empathy in a relationship affects the social circuits of the brain that help create an integrated sense of balance and well-being. Such an imbalance can make you feel isolated and alone. Your mind may become incoherent and your usual sense of vitality drained. The reaction to such feelings can depend on your own makeup: You may become angry and frustrated, or sullen and withdrawn. Or you may find yourself feeling ashamed, as if you have done something wrong and deserve such an experience of being ignored. In these and other common responses, the relationship with a narcissistic individual creates a cascade of neural reactions that are far from the mental well-being associated with coherence of mind and empathy and compassion in relationships. This is a form of stress that you deserve to reduce in your life, even if you cannot change the other person. The knowledge embedded in the pages of this book can serve as a powerful means to help you deal with this stress through insight and information. If you're in any sort of close relationship with a narcissist, you may be in dire need of new ways to understand the situation and respond—for the sake of the health of your mind, your brain, and your relationships.

Fortunately, the advice in this book will guide you through the challenges of both surviving and optimizing a relationship with someone who initially has so little to give, but who often takes so much. At the very least, this guide will help you understand the mechanisms of mind and brain that are at work in your relationship. This alone will help a great deal. But even more, the suggestions here offer the hope of change. With these science-based practical ideas, you may actually open the door to a new way of being—both for you and for the narcissist in your life. Taking the time to dive into these pages and work with the ideas presented will be worth its weight in gold. If relating to a narcissist presents challenges in your life, why not start now? Turn the page and start to learn how you can improve your life.

—Daniel J. Siegel, MD

Author of *Mindsight*, *The Mindful Brain*, and *The Developing Mind* and coauthor of *The Whole-Brain Child* and *Parenting from the Inside Out*

Clinical Professor of Psychiatry, UCLA School of Medicine

Acknowledgments

I would like to gratefully acknowledge the following people, whose love, patience, guidance, and support carried me through this process. I could not have written this book without you.

Momma, you have given me so much strength and the courage to believe in myself. My beautiful Samya "Sweet Pea," you are the light of my life; you are truly amazing and bring so much joy to me and to others. My husband, my dearest David, I am so lucky to have your constant love; thanks for your encouraging and caring words, and for putting up with seeing only the back of my head as I worked on this book. My wonderful Rachel and Ben, you are so special to me. My sister, Lisa, brother-in-law, Arthur, and adorable niece, Cailin ("Miss Munchkin"), you have shown so much kindness and interest in my work. My California family—Dotty, Eliot, Teri, Katie, Jessica, and Isaac—thanks for the many treasures of your love. My cousin MaryLynn, aka "Madame Kukla," you have been a creative and commiserating comrade. My former husband Abdo, thanks for your friendship.

Jack Lagos, thank you for helping me make sense out of my life.

Dr. Aaron T. Beck, how important your contribution to this field—the enormity of your impact is immeasurable. You provided me with an extraordinary foundation in this often complicated profession, giving me a grounded philosophy in which to base my practice.

My dearest friend and mentor, Jeff Young, you have been my greatest inspiration. Your generosity is felt in infinite ways. I have learned so much because of you and your incomparable talent. You've given me not only a brilliant model for working with clients, but also an immense collection of cherished memories. My sweet William Zangwill, you are always there for me with empathy, thoughtfulness, great insight, and the perfect metaphor. My dear friend Cathy Flanagan, your soothing voice and warm heart seem to always show up just when I need them most. Michael First, thank you for your supportive enthusiasm and impeccable diagnostic skills. Thanks also to Maureen Khadder, dear longtime friend and initial collaborator on the idea embodied in this book.

Dan Siegel, mentor and charismatic educator, you've shared your gentleness, your sheer magic, and your lovely sense of humor, along with your unique gift for making dense and difficult material come alive in my brain, adding such an exciting new dimension to my career.

My dear family of colleagues and affiliates of the Cognitive Therapy Center of New Jersey, thank you for tolerating my ups and downs, whining, and celebrating. How fortunate I am to be surrounded by such incredibly bright and supportive people like you: Kathleen Newdeck, Mary Burke, Patrice Fiore, Barbara Levy, Robin Spiro, Kathy Kobberger, Rosemary Erickson, Lissa Parsonnet, Harriet Achtentuch, Margaret Miele, Ava Schlesinger, Paul Schottland, Irv Finklestein, and Bob Jaskiewicz. My Cognitive Therapy Center of New York family, thank you for being such an integral part of my life in so many ways. You are an awesome group of talented and wonderful people: Will Swift, Marty Sloane, Vivian Francesco, Jeff Conway, Travis Atkinson, Merrie Pearl, Pat McDonald, Fred Eberstadt, Lillian and Bob Steinmuller, Mike Minervini, Nancy Ribeiro, Sylvia Tamm, and all the rest of you who have touched my life in so many ways over the years.

Rich Simon, you invited me to write a piece for *Psychotherapy Networker* on this subject, and look what happened! You are an incredible editor who consistently encourages my confidence as a writer.

Tesilya Hanauer, not only did you ask me to write a book for you, but you were continuously there beside me with enthusiasm, support, and brilliant input, never compromising the integrity of my work. This book would not have happened without your initiation and thoughtfulness. Jess Beebe and Nicola Skidmore, along with Tesilya, your superb editing, suggestions, and overall accommodating support have been so immensely appreciated. Jasmine Star, how lucky I am to have been assigned such a warm, talented, and energetic copy editor. You kept my spirits high throughout what is typically a very daunting task. You are a class act! And to all of the staff of New Harbinger Publications and others who worked hard to make my book a success, my deepest thanks.

To the rest of my family and friends, I am so blessed to have the many fortunes of your love. And finally, thank you to my clients; there are so many of you who have been a major source of inspiration to me and to my professional development. I am so grateful for your confidence in me, and for the unparalleled privilege of knowing your stories and witnessing your courage. I am in awe of you. Your openness and your commitment to the painstaking and exhilarating path to personal renewal forever reminds me of why I chose to work in this field.

The revisions and new material in this second edition were written with endless gratefulness for my International Society of Schema Therapy family. Your inspiration and constant support keep the ideas flowing and the creative candle glowing. I would also like to express my immense gratitude to the many readers who have taken the time to write me, offering appreciation, feedback, keen questions, and even critically challenging points of view. All of your thoughtful insights and heartfelt stories have contributed to this second edition of *Disarming the Narcissist*. I thank you for inspiring me to add new and relevant material and elaborations on helpful strategies. I hope you find this edition of the book informative and helpful, and I look forward to your continued feedback.

Introduction

Too often we enjoy the comfort of opinion without the discomfort of thought.

—John F Kennedy

G iven that you're reading this book, it's likely that you're in a relationship with a narcissist, and that this person's excessive self-centeredness and sense of entitlement have hurt you and damaged the relationship time and time again. This book can help. It's filled with useful information, illuminating exercises, and effective strategies. But before I get into the details that will help you understand the narcissist in your life and how you might foster positive changes in your relationship, let's take a quick look at the growing awareness of narcissism and the important role empathy has to play in healing relationships afflicted by narcissistic behaviors.

An Era of Narcissism

In recent years, journalistic reporting on the behavior of notorious silver screen celebrities, sports superstars, and politicians has cast a spotlight on their self-serving lifestyles and "rules don't apply to me" sense of entitlement. In the process, terms and phrases such as "narcissism," "sex addiction," and "lack of empathy" have boldly appeared in the headline of many an article or broadcast (boosting my book sales, thank you very much).

Once limited to psychology textbooks, treatment manuals, and professional dialogues in mental health settings, these expressions are fast becoming familiar within the lexicon of everyday conversation—on social media sites and blogs and in households around the world. As the term "narcissism" has become more widely known and understood, increasing numbers of people are pleased and relieved to finally have a description that fits an obnoxious partner, lover, friend, boss, or family member.

When *Disarming the Narcissist* was first released in 2008, there was little written on the subject for the general reader. The book offered a conceptualized profile of narcissism and strategies that partners and loved ones might use when dealing with a narcissist. I wrote the book largely in response to people who expressed their genuine caring for the narcissist in their lives, despite the challenges—people who wanted to understand their loved one, to influence their loved one to change, and to get their own needs met, if possible.

Given the surge of publicity surrounding narcissism, it isn't surprising that a host of books on this subject have emerged in recent years. Nevertheless, *Disarming the Narcissist* continues to present a unique approach to this challenging issue, offering a comprehensive explanation of narcissism, along with reasonable navigation tools for partners and loved ones, while still recognizing the reality that transformation is likely to be limited at best with this complicated personality type.

The Wisdom of Empathy

The book's approach sometimes raises the ire of my colleagues, clients, and readers as they struggle to integrate their hearts into the matter. Some have said that my book promotes too soft a touch with narcissists and that there is no hope for change with these magisterial maniacs. I certainly understand those feelings; after all, people often find themselves shortchanged and thoroughly frustrated in interactions with narcissists, even after delivering a thoughtful, self-disclosing statement using all of the tools of empathic confrontation and limit setting outlined in this book.

Yet there are potential solutions to this difficult quandary. To gather and maintain momentum with a narcissist using the approach in this book, you must set forth meaningful consequences—something I'll discuss in chapter 7, on empathic confrontation. That brings us to another broad area of misunderstanding and misconception: what, exactly, is empathy, and how could it possibly apply to narcissists? I address this topic briefly a bit later in this introduction and discuss it in detail in chapter 7.

Sometimes a tattered heart and eroded hope don't allow for much patience or the effort required to experiment with different approaches. And, let's face it: It takes more than flawless elocution and carefully crafted language to bring about successful results; it takes leverage and persistence. It also takes a keen understanding of what you're up against, acceptance of the limits and correspondingly adjusted expectations, and a readiness to enforce the consequences. For the therapist, it takes the laser-sharp focus of an Olympic athlete combined with fit emotional muscle, energetic endurance, and the capacity to be vulnerable—to be real, not just nice, and not just smart.

Most books on narcissism urge you to *run, don't walk*—to get away from the me-me-me madman or the vainglorious vamp. But as I've learned while working in support groups with women who have carefully examined this option, it isn't so easy when the narcissist is your spouse and someone you've dedicated decades of your life to, especially if he's the father of your young children. He probably isn't someone you're prepared to hand your little ones over to every other weekend. Nor is it so easy when she's your boss or your eldest daughter and you aren't prepared to exit your job or lose contact with your grandchildren.

Also, it may be that the narcissist is someone you love and understand, someone who captures your heart in brief moments when his vulnerability and humanness manage to sneak out of the imprisonment of ego to occasionally show up as warm and caring—if only for a little while. Sadly, it's always just a matter of time before he appears bored and disinterested. As quickly as he showed up, he'll slip away again. And as he slips away, you may wonder: Does he carry you with him in his mind? Is the representation accurate? Does he get who you are, what you need, and what it feels like to be in your skin? This brings me back to empathy, an often misunderstood and misused term—and one that's particularly puzzling in the context of narcissism. I get a lot of questions about empathy, especially these:

- Isn't "empathy" just another word for "compassion"?

- How can one have empathy for a narcissist?

- Can a narcissist ever truly experience what happens inside another person's skin?

Some of the brightest thinkers and communicators, including journalists, psychologists, researchers, political analysts, anthropologists, and even wordsmiths, are investigating empathy from many angles, from studying mirror neurons to pondering moral consciousness. For example, without empathy or understanding, how can people predict the future, view themselves in comparison to others, and hold the world in their mind?

In response to readers' and clients' quandaries about empathy, and incorporating new findings on this topic, this new edition of *Disarming the Narcissist* contains much more material on the topic, including how empathy promotes emotional stability. This edition also contains new material on the female narcissist in response to a significant number of readers who wrote to me about their struggles with narcissistic mothers, mothers-in-law, sisters, daughters, and wives.

Finally, recognizing that sometimes the best option genuinely is to end the relationship, I've added a new chapter, "Making an Exit: Escaping Perilous Narcissism" (chapter 6). This new chapter specifically addresses the risks and dangers of living with narcissists who demonstrate hazardous behaviors such as aggression, unremitting addictions (including to pornography, infidelity, gambling, and substances), and a missing moral compass combined with remorselessness and an elevated sense of entitlement to do as they please.

Indelible Imprints

My interest in narcissism was seeded by unforgettable experiences with some very difficult clients in my early years of practicing psychotherapy. Armed only with a hazy lingering residue of information from a chapter covered in graduate school, some beginning exposure to the subject in postgraduate studies, and a novice's enthusiasm for the psychology of relationships, I wasn't adequately prepared for dealing with this challenging issue. I found myself flustered, fumbling, and defensive when working with these clients. They could push my buttons like no one else could.

One of my first encounters with a narcissistic client came while I was working as an intern in an organization devoted to family mediation. My job was to conduct interviews with couples in the process of divorcing and assist them in resolving disputes on matters of child custody and visitation. Let's just say that diving into frigid waters headfirst from atop the highest cliff would have been benign in comparison.

My baptism by fire began when an attractive forty-five-year-old man arrived to our session ahead of his soon-to-be ex-wife. He glanced (or glared) at me, a twenty-five-year-old woman in a navy blue suit sporting a clipboard and a welcoming handshake—and with only barely ripened clinical expertise. Without acknowledging me, he took a seat, sighed, looked at his watch, and then asked, "Just exactly how damn long will this nonsense meeting take?" Before I could stutter a response, he asked, "When will the counselor be arriving?" I was always pretty good at staving off color rising toward my face, so with a forced smile I replied, "I am the counselor." He rolled his eyes, threw back his head with disapproval, and turned to stare out the window, impatiently tapping a finger on the arm of his chair.

I'm not sure if it was then or later that evening that I began thinking about a career in floral design, but I was able to tell myself, *Wendy, this is a disgruntled man who is going through a divorce. He has a lot on his mind. He's just upset. You can handle it. You have your inventory of questions, you are rehearsed, and you have an order from the court. Yes, you are uncomfortable with bullies, but you will get through it. You know how to focus, and you are sensitive to your clients.*

His wife arrived about five minutes later—which seemed like days. She was a lovely woman and was immediately apologetic for being late. She introduced herself and said hello to her husband, who didn't respond, and took a seat next to him. I proceeded to open the session by reviewing the information I had received from the court for their verification. He continued to sigh heavily, staring up at the ceiling. She nodded, affirming that all the information was correct.

I then reached the part of the official document that stated the reasons for court-ordered mediation. It said the couple could not agree on who should have primary custody of their three children. He was proposing joint physical custody, and she wanted sole physical custody, granting him reasonable and unlimited visitation. Before I could finish reading the proposal, he interrupted me, rose to his feet, and scowled down at his wife. She immediately dropped her head and fixed her eyes upon the laces of her shoes as he barked, "This is a total waste of time. There will be no mediation. We will go to trial, and then you'll see what you get." Then, looking at me, he continued with, "Put that in your official record, Miss Counselor, and also tell the courts that I am through with this mediation bullshit. She thinks because she is finally getting her happy little divorce that she can have my kids too. Well, we'll see about that. The only way my kids stand a chance of achieving functional brains, and a successful future, is by living with me. Do you know who I am, Miss Counselor? Do you? I am one of the most well-respected litigation attorneys in this state. So…good luck to both of you." With that, he threw his papers on the floor and stalked out.

I believe it was actually at this point that the idea of a career change emerged. The woman cried into her hands. Although I felt like joining her, instead I swallowed the lump in my throat and began to inquire about what just happened. She told me that her husband was, in fact, a very well-known and successful lawyer, and that she would be doomed in trial because of his reputation and his connections. She talked about how his intimidating style had snuffed out the courage—and flattened the egos—of many marriage counselors. No one could hold him accountable.

Her tone seemed sad, and when I told her this, she said that she had been sad for a very long time because her husband was a difficult man, and the product of a very painful childhood. She said that she loved him but just couldn't live with his scorching behaviors anymore, and no one seemed able to help. She was puzzled about how someone who was once a sweet and sensitive little boy could become such an overbearing egotist. We sighed together. I gave her some recommendations for support, and then the session ended. I turned in my noncompliance report, and that was the last I saw of them.

I think about that couple from time to time, wondering if anyone ever reached him, what happened to the children, what happened to her. I vividly remember the snapshot of my unease—my skin temperature rising, my heart rate increasing, my stomach knotting. A love of words, decent communication skills, and a chronic fascination with the human condition—all were silenced by an unfamiliar and shaky sensation of loss of confidence. It was as if that client had stomped out my spunk and compromised my courage. This was the first of several similar sobering experiences in my early career. As my husband always says, "You don't know what you don't know." I had a lot to learn, especially about the complexities of narcissism vis-à-vis interpersonal relationships.

Pivotal Influences

Anyone who knows me knows I have immense curiosity about what makes people tick and a perpetual attraction to understanding it. The necessary decoding of my own emotional assembly has not been exempt. Having spent a good deal of time trying to make sense out of my own makeup, I've come to realize the importance of this commitment and the value of ever-emerging personal discoveries.

More than twenty years ago, I had the good fortune of meeting the incomparable Dr. Jeffrey Young, one of my mentors and also one of my dearest friends. He taught me how to integrate my philosophy of psychotherapy (then, cognitive therapy exclusively) within his richly textured schema therapy model—a superb approach for treating issues of narcissism. I am forever indebted to him for the profoundly important impact he has had, and continues to have, on my life.

In 2003, I was granted another stroke of good luck when I met Dr. Daniel Siegel, the gifted master of interpersonal neurobiology. Under his supervision, I've been able to attach an accessible and user-friendly understanding of the brain to my work. My studies with Dan have been tremendously invigorating and have inspired accelerated movement in therapy with some of my most difficult clients. Bringing the science of the brain on board has strengthened the credibility and validity of the challenging, complex process of dealing with relationships in psychotherapy. It also helps mitigate the shame and stigma associated with seeking help for emotional problems; once clients understand how the brain acts as a residence for experiences and how memory allows access to old painful events, they become less defensive about possibly being labeled "crazy" or "weak." In addition, science removes some of the skepticism that many who enter into therapy may feel. It also helps all of us appreciate the important workings of our fundamental biology and how this is integrated with our life experiences.

Shared Wisdom

It has been many years since that painful meeting in the family mediation office. I have spent a lot of time struggling, experimenting, studying, and carving my niche. Now, ironically, I am considered to be an expert in narcissism, having worked with this population and their "victims" for years now. My client population mostly comprises narcissistic men, a lesser number of narcissistic women, and people who are trying to cope with narcissists in their lives. I'm not sure how to explain this passion. My colleagues tend to scratch their heads. They find it a bit unusual, even masochistic, as most clinicians shudder at the thought of working with narcissists and many will not accept referrals of this type. All I can say is that it has become very satisfying in terms of my personal growth and in my work as a therapist and an educator.

Not every narcissist is willing to change, but some will—with enough leverage, incentive, and assistance. However, that's not the goal of this book. Rather, it is intended to help those who are trying to deal with a narcissistic person. It will define and illustrate different types of narcissism, offer explanations for why and how narcissism develops as part of a person's personality, and provide guidance and tools for effectively surviving and even thriving in relationships with these challenging folks. It will also help you identify your own life patterns and personal life themes so that you can understand why you may be drawn to narcissistic people, and why you get uncomfortable and stuck when dealing with them. It will help you develop a reflective and sturdy voice when communicating with the narcissist in your life about realistic intentions, needs, and expectations. This book is designed to assist you not only in getting through the difficult challenges, but also in achieving improved and more satisfying experiences when interacting with a narcissist.

One thing to note at the outset is that almost all experts in the field agree that more than 75 percent of narcissists are male (and for this reason, I've used the male pronoun more often in this book). This is partly attributed to gender-related qualities, such as aggression, competitiveness, limited attachment to others, dominance, and societal norms, particularly as they apply to nature versus nurture issues in child development. Women can be narcissistic too, but they tend to express these traits mostly within the domains of personal appearance or vanity, the status of their children or household, and their value as caregivers. In addition, narcissistic women are inclined toward more covert manifestations of this syndrome. They are likely to show up as martyrs, whiners, and gratuitous victims. Of course, you will also meet grand dames and divas, who look more like their male counterparts in their aggressive quest for attention and admiration.

The similarity between male and female narcissists is that both are distracted by an insatiable need to be the center of attention, whether this is expressed overtly or discreetly. This limits, or even eliminates, their capacity to be empathic and remorseful. You may have heard the term "narcissistic injury." This refers to the dynamic wherein, for a narcissist, saying a simple "I'm sorry" is like saying, "I am the worst human being on earth." For all their bravado, they are easily injured by criticism, others' disappointment in them, differing points of view, lack of notice or compliments, being ignored, and even their own mistakes. But you won't necessarily know they are feeling injured, because they are masterful cover-up artists. Instead of appearing wounded, they will hurl the prickliest words at you, avoid you, or demand your applause for some other part of their wonderfulness. You may find yourself surrendering, offering an "I'm sorry" of your own in an effort to quell their unrelenting reactions and mend their tattered egos.

But it need not be this way. It is possible to maintain your own composure and self-esteem when dealing with narcissistic people. The first step is to develop an understanding of narcissism and how it arises —the topic of chapter 1. This can help you realize that the interpersonal issues between the two of you aren't necessarily about you. It can also help you discover empathy and, in some cases, even compassion for the narcissist in your life, bringing you more peace of mind and potentially improving your relationship.

chapter 1

Framing the Situation: Toward an Understanding of Narcissism

The mass of men lead lives of quiet desperation.

—Henry David Thoreau

The narcissist both appeals and appalls. He may look like a modern-day Sir Lancelot, replete with the most swaggering charm one could imagine and adorned in the shining armor of our time: a handsome portfolio and dazzling acquisitions. Beware! This knight is a master of illusion. In fact, he can be downright menacing. You may fall prey to the seductive lure of his accomplishments, intelligence, and seemingly flawless self-confidence. However, his arrogance, condescension, sense of entitlement, and lack of empathy are formidable offenders that inevitably lead to frustrating interpersonal encounters and chronically difficult long-term relationships.

She may be found decorated in the trendiest of glad rags, strutting along the corridors of some corporate headquarters armed with an attaché, monopolizing the floor at a Monday night parent-teacher meeting, or delegating duties at a community service gathering. She may also bear a striking resemblance to the woman on the cover of the latest domestic diva magazine, decked out in a push-up bra while sporting the consumer's most highly recommended quick-and-easy floor mop. This gal does it all, and she'll be the first to let you know that: "Well, I don't mean to brag, but…" Or "I don't mean to complain, but…" Or "I can't think of another woman who would put up with…"

She may even be married to the previously described wiling warrior. Her needs, gallantly subjugated to his towering prowess, are only shared with those who will stroke her selflessness and provide her with an awe-filled "I don't know how you do it." Indeed, this lovely yet unabashed matron of martyrdom craves applause even as her self-effacing wisdom and perfectly perky posture leave us squirming, as if listening to the screech of nails on a chalkboard.

The Narcissist at a Glance

What I've learned from over twenty years of experience working with these types of people is that there are few challenges in psychotherapy greater than treating the narcissist. This is the client who has come into therapy because a partner finally mustered up the courage to say, "Get help or get out." Or perhaps his boss gave him an ultimatum based upon countless complaints about his difficult attitude. Maybe he's losing momentum in his competitive stride to the top and is looking for an edge. He may be involved in a litigious matter and believe that counseling might look good in his file. Occasionally, and reluctantly, narcissists enter into therapy because they are simply lonely, depressed, or anxious.

So what do we call this personality type, the one that throws you off balance with curious paradoxes of character? Though these people seem well-assembled and self-assured, sometimes with a saccharine wit, they can so quickly pull the rug out from under you, reducing you to apprehension, tears, boredom, or disgust. We call these people narcissists. (As mentioned in the introduction, the majority of narcissist are male, so I'll primarily use the male pronoun and male examples throughout this book; however, at the end of this chapter you'll find material on particularities of female narcissists.)

Exercise: Is the Difficult Person in Your Life a Narcissist?

Read through the items listed below and check off any that apply to the difficult person in your life. Only check off a trait if it is expressed excessively, meaning it occurs more often than not. (This exercise is also available for download at www.newharbinger.com/27602. See back of book for more information.)

___✓___ Self-absorbed (acts like everything is all about him or her)

___✓___ Entitled (makes the rules and breaks the rules)

___✓___ Demeaning (puts you down and is bullyish)

___✓___ Demanding (demands whatever he or she wants)

_____ Distrustful (is suspicious of your motives when you're being nice to him or her)

___✓___ Perfectionistic (has rigidly high standards; things are done his or her way or no way)

___✓___ Snobbish (believes he or she is superior to you and others; gets bored easily)

___✓___ Approval seeking (craves constant praise and recognition)

___✓___ Unempathic (is uninterested in understanding your inner experience or unable to do so)

___✓___ Unremorseful (cannot offer a genuine apology)

___✓___ Compulsive (gets overly consumed with details and minutiae)

___✓___ Addictive (cannot let go of bad habits; uses them to self-soothe)

_____ Emotionally detached (steers clear of feelings)

If you checked at least ten of the thirteen traits, the difficult person in your life most likely meets the criteria for overt maladaptive narcissism, the most common and difficult form. This type of narcissist is in your face and unwieldy. I call it overt maladaptive narcissism to differentiate it from other forms of narcissism, such as covert maladaptive narcissism and healthy narcissism, which I'll discuss a little later. The terms "overt" and "maladaptive" are combined here to mean an observable inability to adequately fit in, conform, or adjust to conditions in the environment or basic expectations within relationships. If the narcissist in your life is, in fact, truly an overt maladaptive narcissist, don't despair. You already knew you had your hands full. You may not have known what to call this person, and you probably haven't known what to do about it. But you're getting closer. Read on.

If you've checked a lesser number of items on the list, you may be dealing with a challenging but less obstreperous narcissist. Narcissism appears along a spectrum, going from healthy narcissism at one end to overt and covert maladaptive narcissism at the other. I'll define all of these different types in this chapter.

What Is a Narcissist?

The term "narcissism" hails from Greek mythology's tale of Narcissus, who was doomed to eternally fall in love with his own image in a mountain pool as punishment for refusing to accept an offer of love by Echo, a young mountain nymph. Because Narcissus could only crave but never actually possess the image he saw reflected in the pool, he simply pined away and was eventually turned into a beautiful flower. The evocative tragedy in this myth provides us with the moral that true beauty and lovability blossom when obsessive and excessive self-love expires.

Narcissists are often self-absorbed and preoccupied with a need to achieve the perfect image (recognition, status, or being envied) and have little or no capacity for listening, caring, or understanding the needs of others. This self-absorption can leave them without a true and intimate connection to others—one that offers a feeling of being understood and being held safely and lovingly in the mind and heart of another person. Such connections allow us to experience the difference between love of self and love of another. Learning how to balance self-directed attention with other-directed attention is an important part of childhood development. It is a fundamental tutorial for life, fostering the development of reciprocity, responsibility, and empathy with others. Unfortunately, it is sorely lacking in the narcissist's early development.

The narcissist may journey through life sporting a brash and stridently boastful ego while unknowingly yearning, like all of us, for the uniquely quiet and safe refuge found within a heartfelt human embrace. While you may experience the narcissist as having little or no regard for your needs and feelings, as someone only willing to garner your attention through a self-absorbed sense of entitlement and obnoxiousness, the truth is that he actually longs for a deeper and much more profound connection—a need that he simply cannot realize, comprehend, or accept. He's likely to view the idea of an emotionally intimate connection as weak and pathetic. As a consequence of his unrealized longings, which he considers unacceptable, his needs are misguided, so he can only seek your attention through charming yet unnerving behaviors.

Origins of Narcissism

Once upon a time, this competitive braggart was simply a little child who had wants, needs, and feelings, just like every child who enters the world. What could have led that child down a path toward an assumed rightful placement on center stage, beneath the spotlight of specialness, where the rules apply to others but not to him? Let's take a look at a few possible explanations.

The Spoiled Child

One theory suggests that a narcissist may have grown up in a home where the notion of being better than others and having special rights and privileges was indoctrinated and modeled. This was typically a home where few limits were set and no significant consequences were assigned for overstepping boundaries or breaking rules. His parents may not have adequately taught him how to manage or tolerate discomfort. He may have been utterly indulged. This sort of dynamic primed him for reenactments in adulthood and set the stage for the development of the purely spoiled narcissist.

The Dependent Child

Another proposal is that one or both parents may have been overly involved in making the child's life as pain-free as possible. Instead of teaching and encouraging the child to develop age-appropriate skills for managing tasks and social interactions, his parents may have done everything for him. As a result, he was robbed of a sense of personal competence and learned instead that he was helpless and dependent. He may have grown up feeling entitled to have others take care of everything so he wouldn't have to face dealing with frustration or the potential humiliation of making a bad decision or feeling like a failure.

The Lonely, Deprived Child

The most popular proposal for the typical origins of narcissism is that the child grew up feeling conditionally loved, meaning that love was based upon performance. His parents may have expected him to be the best, instilling the message that being anything short of perfect meant he was flawed, inadequate, and unlovable. He may have been taught that love is tentative and contingent. He may have been manipulated into believing that he could get his emotional needs met if he strived for greatness. His parents may have sought their own sense of pride and attention through his achievements, implying that he was forbidden to embarrass them with less-than-perfect performance.

This scenario may be complicated by different treatment from each parent. These children are often criticized by one parent and made to feel that whatever they do is never really good enough. They may then be doted on, overprotected, or used as a surrogate spouse by the other parent. They may be compliant with their parents' demands and expectations as a means of receiving their limited attention and dodging criticism and shame. In response to this profound emotional deprivation, manipulation, and control, and the stifling of his precious and vulnerable little self, the child develops an approach to life characterized by such principles as *I will need no one*, *No one is to be trusted*, *I will take care of myself*, or *I'll show you*.

He was not loved for being the boy he was, and was neither guided nor encouraged in the discovery of his true inclinations. He was not held in the arms of a caregiver who would make him feel completely safe and unquestionably cherished. He was not shown how to walk in someone else's shoes, or how to feel the inner emotional life of another person. There was no role model for this in his experience, where personal interactions were devoid of empathy. He was instead ridden with shame and a sense of defectiveness, both from the direct criticism and from the withholding of emotional nourishment and, often, physical affection. He was made to feel there was something wrong with him, as if he was weak for wanting comfort and attention. In defense, he mustered up whatever safeguards he could in order to extinguish the pain associated with these life themes.

The Mixed Bag

You might also find that "his majesty" and "her highness" are best described by a combination of the origins proposed above. Given the complexity of human interactions (and reactions), it's hardly surprising that people come by their character as a result of a combination of factors, rather than a single factor.

Spoiled-dependent. The narcissist in your life might best be characterized as having been spoiled as well as dependent. In this case, not only will he act entitled and feel superior (not surprising given the family modeling of a "we're better than others" attitude), he may also feel dependent and incompetent, as his parents were always waiting on him and rescuing him instead of helping him develop the necessary skills of self-reliance and functionally appropriate dependence. As an adult, he may show up as entitled and expect to be doted on and indulged. Or he may avoid taking initiative and making decisions because he has an underlying fear of shamefully exposing his limitations and failures when tackling the everyday decisions of life.

Deprived-dependent. Another combination that might characterize your narcissist is being both a deprived type and a dependent type. In this case he will be easily offended as well as dependent, needing others to constantly reassure him that he is great and manage life for him. Discreetly, he seeks out others to protect him from a deeply felt sense of shame about his defective, lonely, and inadequate self. He may come across as needy and hypersensitive, rather than demanding and show-offish. He may show signs of being addicted to self-soothing behaviors, such as working, spending, gambling, pornography, overeating, and so on. You might refer to him as a high-maintenance type. And while he may have a longer fuse, beware. When he's forced to face the frustration of a challenging task or finds himself the butt of one too many jousts in verbal repartee, his sensitivity to feeling foolish and defective may either launch him into the tyrannical state of meanness typical of narcissists or cause him to disappear within his stonewalled, silent abyss.

While some experts speculate that the manifestations of narcissism may grow out of biologically determined personality traits, most feel that they arise due to a combination of the child's early experiences and biological makeup, or temperament. It's important to note that many children grow up in environments like those described above without becoming narcissistic. These children may have experienced a different outcome because of a more stable temperament, a loving grandparent who filled the void, or perhaps a teacher, caregiver, or other role model who helped instill healthy and adaptive disciplinary tools. It is usually the case that biological and environmental influences interact with each other in creating personality and character.

Exercise: What Type of Narcissist Are You Dealing With?

Think about the narcissist you're dealing with. See if you can identify his or her type from the lists of behaviors below. Check off any tendencies that pertain to the narcissist in your life. (Of course, if you know this person's childhood history, you may already have some helpful clues.) This exercise will help you identify the most popular forms of narcissism, especially the deprived type. However, there can be a great deal of individual variation in traits and states. If your narcissist doesn't fit neatly into the categories below, he or she may be more purely the spoiled type or dependent type.

Spoiled-Dependent

_____ Speaks as if he or she is superior to others, whether in terms of looks, intelligence, accomplishments, or other regards. (Example: "After all, I *do* have an Ivy League education.")

_____ Expects special attention from almost everyone or acts as though the rules don't apply to him or her. (Example: "What do you mean, I have to *wait* to be seated?!")

_____ Interrupts others when they are speaking, assuming that his or her words are of much greater import. (Example: "No, no, the real issue is…")

_____ Prone to temper tantrums or avoidance when he or she can't figure something out or things don't go his or her way. (Example: "What do you mean you didn't make the reservations? I insisted on going to Cafe Grande!")

✓ Speaks in long-winded monologues and views himself or herself as an expert on everything who should not be interrupted. (Examples: "What I think is…" "My opinion is…" "So, as I've told you,…blah, blah, blah.")

Deprived-Dependent

_____ Constantly fishing for compliments, recognition, and favors; feels insecure and inadequate underneath the appearance of a sturdy facade. (Examples: "So you really liked what I did, didn't you?" "Looks good on me, don't you think?")

✓ Demands explanations and clarification in conversations; often feels that people are trying to hurt, humiliate, or take advantage of him or her. (Examples: "What exactly are you saying about me?" "Are you calling me a liar?" "So now you think nothing I do is good enough?")

✓ Turns on you or hides when frustrated or hurt; feels entitled to protecting his or her ego through attack, distraction, or consumption. (Examples: "How dare you!" "What can I expect, given your limitations." "I'll show you." Works excessively, overeats, gets overly busy with projects that never get completed, compulsively surfs the Internet, drinks too much, has affairs, spends excessive amounts of money.)

Review the items you marked and notice if your narcissist fits more into the spoiled-dependent category or the deprived-dependent one. Alternatively, you may find that he or she has all or almost all of the traits from both categories. This probably indicates the classic origins of narcissism: the lonely, deprived child. Such people tend to harbor the tendencies listed above and deploy them under certain conditions reminiscent of their childhood.

If your narcissist is the spoiled-dependent type, change will require placing more emphasis on setting limits. The narcissist will also need to enroll in some lessons about tolerating frustration. For the deprived-dependent type, you'll need to place more emphasis on ignoring boastful commentaries and instead pay attention to the narcissist's "ordinary" niceties and thoughtful gestures. Such people will also need to be held accountable for angry outbursts and be encouraged to develop reflective self-regulating tools for calming overly reactive anger. Establishing collaborative exit strategies, such as time-outs, will also be helpful.

Of course, the causative factors and problematic behaviors will be unique to each individual, requiring a tailored approach. I'll elaborate on these issues and change strategies, as well as other interventions for change, in later chapters.

The Magician: Disappearing When It's Time to Focus on You

The narcissist is on a constant quest for first place in the race for supreme emotional autonomy, meaning that he needs no one and only has himself to count on. His personal longings and hardships are typically well concealed beneath a cloak of success, power, competitiveness, righteousness, or some combination thereof. He might be the glory seeker, the contester, or the perennial master of ceremonies. Perhaps he is always ready to rescue the damsel in distress, to persist in proving a point of view until you scream uncle, or to entertain you with name-dropping, storytelling, or a litany of clever and impressive metaphors. However, his emotional illiteracy, due to his detachment and hyperautonomy, limits his capacity for empathy or precludes it all together.

When you are in an exchange with an empathic person, you know it because you have the feeling that the person truly gets you. Empathic people seem to understand your feelings and your experience, even if they have a different point of view. Empathy, this felt sense of the other, is the ability and the willingness to imagine walking in the other person's shoes. It can be differentiated from sympathy in that it is not simply feeling sorrow for another's pain, it is the art of tuning in to it, allowing it to resonate within your own body and mind. It is one of the most powerfully connective qualities of a healthy relationship, and its absence can be devastating. Daniel Goleman, in his book *Social Intelligence* (2006), suggests that someone who doesn't empathize with others can treat them as objects rather than as people.

Now You See Him, Now You Don't

The narcissist's lack of empathy can manifest in different ways. For example, if you are finally able to wedge a word into a conversation with a narcissist, asking him to tune in to your world, he's likely to suddenly become the amazing Houdini, disappearing before your very eyes. He may literally walk away in the middle of your sentence or announce an important "something" that he must get to right away. While a female narcissist may do this, it's more likely to occur with a male narcissist.

And when life presents you with a more critical condition, such as a health problem or other personal crisis, the narcissist becomes more entrenched in his absence. Suddenly you find yourself needing to focus on yourself, perhaps fighting for your life or the life of a loved one, yet the now "inconvenienced" you know who becomes even more unbelievably obnoxious, unhelpful, selfish, or checked out. When my dad was very ill and eventually dying, my self-sacrificing clients actually felt guilty coming in for their sessions, despite my repeated reassurance that I really wanted to be there for them. On the other hand, my narcissistic clients often seemed visibly annoyed if I arrived at a session a little late after leaving the hospital.

Hiding Behind the Armor of Coping Modes

The narcissist's reactions are swift and diverse. He may try to make you feel foolish and unreasonable for making a request or voicing a complaint by putting you down for your "silly" emotional needs. He may talk over you with an insistent (and avoidant) soliloquy on the differences between apples and oranges, wants and needs, Plato and Aristotle, Democrats and Republicans, or any number of other non sequiturs. A narcissist in a coping mode is essentially hiding.

He may offer you a reply along the lines of "I don't know what you want from me," then point out all the ways in which he is the greatest and above reproach. Narcissists consistently hide their insecurities so that no one can hurt, humiliate, disappoint, or use them again. However, hiding behind this false bravado means they forfeit many intimate joys and sorrows and, along with them, many of their heart's desires.

If you're in a romantic relationship with a narcissist, he may feel the threatening emergence of that lonely little child the minute you ask him for a tour of his inner emotional domain, or even when you invite him to wander through yours. It's likely that he fears making contact with the child, viewing him as a defective, lonely, and shameful little pest, so he'll push him ever deeper out of his awareness in any way he can. In so doing, he pushes you away as well. This absence of emotional intimacy can leave you experiencing loneliness, even when the narcissist is right beside you.

A client who was married to a narcissistic man said that she found herself less lonely when he traveled than when he was at home in the same room with her. She had no expectations when he was away, whereas when he was home, his inability to be emotionally available left her feeling far more lonely and deprived. He, unfortunately, was immersed in an evasive strategy of emotional silence. To him, any exposure of his vulnerability would feel like a fusing of the two of them in some needy and dependent way. This is unthinkable for the narcissist, whose mission is one of sovereign self-reliance.

Marion Solomon, PhD, director of clinical training at the Lifespan Learning Institute, writes in her book *Narcissism and Intimacy* (1992) that the narcissist fears the loss of a sense of self when entering an emotional merger. For narcissists, intimacy feels like a stifling and dangerous dwelling.

The Mantras: His and Hers

I will need no one is the resounding and self-affirming mantra of the narcissist, particularly for male narcissists. *You owe me* is more often the female narcissist's recurring refrain. These underlying themes are, of course, completely outside of the narcissist's awareness—an automatic tune that plays repeatedly in the background thanks to well-grooved memories. This intricate memory system is also where self-preserving well-worn masks that assist in coping reside.

The Masks

The narcissist's masks allow him to transform potentially painful states into a bearable, perhaps even comfortable experience. Donning a mask is a way to shift into another form of being when faced with uncomfortable, upsetting feelings. These masks might be viewed as a metaphor for protection, also known as a coping mode.

A mode is simply a state of being. We all shift from mode to mode. For example, one moment you may be in a giving and self-sacrificing mode and the next moment find yourself shifting into a lonely and vulnerable mode. Here are some of the most common modes, or masks, of the narcissist:

- The bully

- The show-off

- The addictive self-soother

- The entitled one

Chapter 5 provides a more detailed discussion of each of these masks and explains how to effectively deal with them. Other masks the narcissist might adopt are the workaholic, the rescuer, and the morally righteous martyr. The strategies offered for the four most common masks can be adapted to deal with the others.

The Narcissist's Strategy for Dealing with Unmet Needs

Based on their implicit and explicit memories of unmet childhood needs, many narcissists develop the notion that such needs will never be met later on in life. This fear is at the root of the narcissist's flimsy and unanimated attachments to others. He compensates for the fear of not having his needs met through a well-executed excessively autonomous style. This combination of fear and overcompensation also leads to a lack of intimacy with himself, a void of self-knowing.

When a narcissist tries to escape these difficult feelings, he may automatically shift into one of the coping modes listed above, donning whatever mask best suits his needs in the situation. These maladaptive coping modes produce some of the characteristically negative behaviors you may be experiencing with the narcissist in your life. Unfortunately, these masks actually perpetuate the feelings he seeks to avoid, re-creating the all-too-familiar shame, loneliness, mistrust, and deprivation of his early experiences. For example, in an effort to not feel his awkwardness in a social setting, he will complain of being bored or will launch into one of his grandstanding monologues on some piece of esoteric wisdom. Consequentially, he will appear not only awkward, but rude and obnoxious as well.

Jeffrey Young, founder of schema therapy (which we'll explore in chapter 2) and an expert on narcissism, writes about the high costs of hiding one's true self: loss of joy, spontaneity, trust, and intimacy (Young and Klosko 1994). He describes how the narcissist may look fine on the surface of his false self, but underneath he still feels defective and unloved.

Covert Narcissism

Now and then, narcissists show up in camouflaged packaging and proceed to impress you with grandiloquent, if subtle, nobility. These morally self-righteous martyrs are forever pointing out the "right" and "wrong" way of living in the world. They are forever differentiating themselves from "prejudiced people" and those who are "selfish and lazy." Quick to the rescue, covert narcissists are eager to find solutions to all of your problems. They will spout their philosophy on the salvation of your soul—speaking with "should" and "must," "always" and "never," and "all or nothing" and proclaiming how the world would be a better place if people just paid attention and followed the rules (their rules, of course!).

The covert narcissist proudly declares an allegiance to the truth. He offers his undeniable humbleness and human imperfection in an effort to impress you. Behind this thin veil, he modestly confesses his loyalty to rigorous self-improvement. He might say, "Sure, I could talk about the ten-thousand-dollar donation I made to the humanitarian foundation, but I'm not that kind of person. I don't need praise for my philanthropic calling."

The covert narcissist can hide behind a facade of morally upstanding servitude for a while, but just wait. Like all narcissists, he hungers for glorified recognition, so it's just a matter of time before he is captured by the throbbing pain of the deprived and lonely child within, who longs to be noticed in a special way. He tucks that annoying child back inside himself and reveals his ravenous appetite for recognition as an extraordinary human being—not an ordinary terrestrial, but something more akin to an archangel. With little tolerance for his simple longings for love and connection and little confidence in the possibility of achieving love and connection, the narcissist reaches for grand recognition and approval in a quest to affirm his prominently declared emotional independence.

It is particularly difficult for him to escape the pain he feels when the honors being granted to him for his generosity aren't spectacular enough or the spotlight fades too quickly. In time, resentment and frustration about his giving and doing, and lack of continuous praise, jiggles the tightrope of his seemingly tidy and stoic disposition and down he falls, landing upon whomever happens to be in his path. You may find yourself the subject of his cold eyes, upturned nose, and clenched brow. You may be treated to an artful diatribe on the ungrateful and imbecilic nature of people and bureaucracies. He spews because he is disappointed at receiving less than a five-minute standing ovation for his performance in the public eye. He counterattacks the perceived enemies of his ego with smug gestures or lambasting commentaries, and through this tantrum-like retort, he hoists himself back up on his self-righteous throne.

The Difference between Male and Female Narcissists

Many traits are common to both male and female narcissists. Both can be identified by their love affair with the sound of their own voice and their ceaseless search for undying admiration. Both will assault you with their opinions, complaints, and criticisms until your very last nerve is frayed or you are bored to tears. If you try to wedge a word in edgewise while they're delivering a monologue, you'll suddenly become invisible. They only have ears for the rising crescendo of their lofty vocals or your admiration and are deaf to anything you might contribute to the conversation. All they can see in that shiny, glazed-over look on your face is their own reflection. And because they have yet to develop the capacity for empathy, they don't understand that their efforts to impress you and snag your applause are actually flooding you with fantasies of an emergency alarm or any sudden interruption that might allow you a prompt exit from their oppressive entrapment.

Because the majority of narcissists are male, the examples in this chapter—and throughout the book—tend to focus on how narcissism manifests in men. Chapter 6, on some of the most damaging types of narcissistic behavior, relates entirely to male narcissists. However, 20 to 25 percent of the type of narcissists examined in this book are female, and they tend to have different characteristics. So let's go ahead and take a look at what distinguishes these divas, drama queens, grand dames, prima donnas, femme fatales, and matrons of martyrdom from their male counterparts.

"Narcissisters": The Lowdown on Her Highness

The female narcissist may be a temptress who beseeches you with saucy sauntering. Alternatively, she may wither you with her self-effacing sanctimony and envy-radiating, disapproving glare. A particularly common type of female narcissist is the victim or martyr: She might capture you with her exasperated "I'm everything to everyone" discourse on how much she does, has to do, and has done and won't be appreciated for. This virtuoso victim is seldom more than half a breath away from her next emotive purge. Should you mention that you aren't feeling well or that you're running late for an appointment, she won't miss a beat; your needs will vanish within the gravity well of her vast self-importance.

Mired in her martyrdom, she will keenly sense it if you dare to disagree with or ignore her, and she'll make you pay by pouting, sobbing, or maybe even threatening to abandon you or hurt herself. It can sometimes feel like you've been granted the supporting actor role in a low-budget movie: She might drop to the couch, clutching her chest and complaining of a sharp pain. Reduced to fear, you may offer a groveling apology and promise to attend to her more closely. You may recant your opinions and agree with her. You may offer excuses, saying you must be tired or distracted and weren't thinking clearly. You may even praise her for her graciousness and thank her for giving you a second chance.

If you haven't dealt with this type of narcissist, that may sound like an overdone melodramatic moment. But it's exactly the scene described to me by Bob, a client who contacted me about his narcissistic bride-to-be. He was so alarmed by her chest pains that he called 911 because he thought she was having a heart attack—much to the shock and embarrassment of his fiancée.

The narcissister will have your mind bending like a contortionist. Should you fight to squelch her fiery theatrics and salvage your sanity, she will gradually shift into a pageantry of pouts, sniffles, and sassy smugness. Yes, she has your numbers on speed dial: self-doubt, guilt, and rejection. And this narcissister will get you to answer her call every time.

Narcissistic Mothers

When the queen in question happens to be your mother, it tends to up the ante. One client shared an incident where she and her mother were sitting in lawn chairs at an outdoor concert when her mom looked at her, shielding her eyes, and said, "Change seats with me, Deborah. The sun is in my eyes." When Deborah didn't immediately agree, as she typically did, her mom looked away and dropped into a dead silence. It may sound like a small incident, but it was just one in a lifetime of similar instances where the ice queen put her own needs before those of her child.

Given that growing up with a narcissistic parent can be a strong predictor for the development of narcissistic traits, you may wonder how Deb was spared from developing a narcissistic personality herself. As stated earlier, temperament, mood, emotional and behavioral inclinations, and environmental influences are all factors in shaping the personality of the child. As a young girl, Deb was inhibited and anxious, startled easily, and often felt guilty when her mom was upset. It isn't uncommon for children of narcissistic parents, especially female children, to become firmly indoctrinated with the belief that it's their job to make the parent happy and that it's their fault when the parent is upset.

In Deb's case, it was a natural response to her mom's repeated distress siren: "You should be ashamed of yourself, young lady. Don't you dare embarrass me! You ingrate! After all I've done for you... You're such a disappointment. What a bad mother I must be (whimper, pout, sniffle)." In addition, Deb's father was extremely self-sacrificing and intimidated by his wife. In the service of peace at any price, he always agreed with or gave in to his wife. It's no wonder that Deb picked up some cues from his modeling, especially given the limited power children have and their desire for stability, safety, love, and acceptance.

Vanity Thy Name Is...

Narcissistic women tend to place more importance on their physical appearance than narcissistic men do, flaunting their bodily attributes (and often augmentations). "Mirror, mirror on the wall..." is the mantra of the femme fatale. Female narcissists also tend to place more emphasis on having a high fashion IQ, trendy decor, and children who are meticulously accessorized for success, socially or academically, than male narcissists do. In this technologic age of "your business is everyone's business," an explanation for this surge in status-matters might be simply competitive stereotypical gender socialization gone wild.

Blogger Susan Walsh (2010) makes some interesting observations about this phenomenon: "During the 70s and 80s, Americans became obsessed with celebrity culture, and eating disorders skyrocketed. Today, social media breeds narcissism by constantly encouraging women to post flattering photos and create online profiles that stress their uniqueness. [Social media sites] require self-promotion, bringing out the narcissist in us. Reality shows promote the most ordinary, unimpressive people as special, and we follow their dysfunctional lives with fascination.... Female narcissists see their lives as a running feature film with them in the lead, receiving accolades at all times."

In an era of young girls clad in pink "Princess" T-shirts, a worrisome message emerges. That we have cause for concern is backed up by data on narcissism from surveys of college students and young adults indicating a culture of specialness and entitlement. It seems that more and more young women (and men) are adopting a disturbing ideology of self-government that I refer to as a narcisstocracy. Under this self-serving administration, they come to believe that the only things that matter in life are looking great, excelling in performance and achievement, winning the attention of important people, and positioning themselves well, and that if they do these things, the world will come right to their door. They aren't concerned about the needs of others or the impact of their behavior on others unless it stymies their winner-take-all ambition, and gets in the way of getting what they want. Most importantly, and so different from the compensatory type that often cloaks the self-doubting, insecure vulnerability of the narcissist, this growing breed is marinated in a saucy blend of sugary specialness and spicy entitlement.

Healthy Narcissism

Narcissism sounds like a disaster, doesn't it? But is narcissism always bad? Actually, it's not. Healthy narcissism contains the seeds of assertiveness and self-respect. While "healthy narcissism" sounds like an oxymoron, in reality narcissism occurs along a spectrum within the human condition. Embodied in human nature itself is a tendency for narcissistic expression. And that isn't all bad.

Healthy Childhood Narcissism

If you delve into the literature on childhood development, you'll learn that nearly every child comes into the world with the capacity to be impulsive, angry, and demanding (as well as joyful, playful, and curious). These qualities are simply elements of the broad spectrum of emotions linked to a child's natural vulnerability and innate temperament. Narcissism has robust value for children. It helps them express their physical and emotional discomfort, especially in the preverbal years. The child becomes angry, cries, and demands attention in order to obtain protection, approval, comfort, and playful engagement. This is healthy and developmentally appropriate behavior.

A wise and loving approach to parenting seeks to provide the emotional and physical support that will allow the child to become secure and competent. It works to provide reasonable limits in order to promote safety and tolerance. It tries to foster a healthy balance between receptivity to others and self-directed attention. Most parents hope their children will grow up with wise and loving internal advocates and a healthy sense of entitlement, meaning they will maintain their sense of self-worth and recognize that they have a right to be respected and included. Parents also want their children to gain an appreciation and respect for the rights of others. And they must attempt to do all of this against the backdrop of the many unsolved mysteries of parenting, their own lingering issues, and their child's unique temperament. This can surely be a challenging and possibly daunting task for any parent.

In *Parenting from the Inside Out* (Siegel and Hartzell 2004), Daniel Siegel writes about the need for parents to make sense of their own early life experiences and to create healthy and coherent personal narratives so they can provide effective modeling and attuned communication and raise children who will thrive. Parents who learn how to connect the dots of their own journey through life have a heightened chance of offering loving and skillful discipline to their children.

In a loving and grounded parent-child relationship, the notion of shame can play an appropriate role in discipline as a means of calibrating the barometer of give-and-take and teaching the child a sense of family values and personal responsibility without implying that the child is bad and unlovable. With this approach, the child learns how to be accountable without feeling flawed and damaged. The goal is to create a home where the child learns to celebrate her creativity and self while also developing a sense of responsibility to the community of others. As the gifted poet and philosopher John O'Donohue said, "A home is a place where a set of different destinies begin to articulate and define themselves. It is the cradle of one's future" (2000, 31).

In summary, healthy childhood narcissism evolves into integrity—the art of making a promise and keeping it. It harnesses an authentic picture of the child, not a cloaked one. It enables the child to articulate her intentions, needs, and purpose in the world with clarity and sensitivity to others. Healthy narcissism allows for a sturdier and more secure attachment to others, promoting sentiments of responsibility and reciprocity.

Healthy Adult Narcissism

When considering the term "healthy adult narcissism," you may think of a particular person who has achieved a degree of fame or recognition and who is currently making a difference in the community or in the world. This person may also be having a profoundly personal impact on your life. People who exhibit healthy adult narcissism may or may not have been fortunate enough to receive all the gifts of wise and loving parenting and a stable and healthy home in which to grow and evolve. Their beginnings may have been stormy and turbulent, and their life journey may have taken them across rough terrain or through quagmires. They may have come by the qualifier "healthy" through therapy, spiritual guidance, or any number of self-help practices. They may have been healed by the gentle kindness of a teacher, a friend, a mentor, or a lover.

While positions of success and celebrity are often prominently held by odious and challenging people with overt maladaptive narcissism, many successful people inhabit the domain of well-adjusted, or healthy, narcissism. Why do we still need to use the term "narcissism" with this group? In part, it's because these people, who often possess above-average dexterity and prowess, aren't like the ordinary "nice guy" when it comes to self-esteem and their facility for dealing with opponents.

Oprah Winfrey, like other icons of the media, makes us feel grateful for healthy adult narcissism. Without it, the eye-opening issues and lessons of transformation that emerge from her provocative interviews might not reach our awareness and mobilize our senses. Through keen-edged, frank, and sometimes prickly confrontations, viewers come to witness missions of hope, humility, and possibility and develop a profound connection to personal responsibility.

So how might we characterize healthy adult narcissists? Typically, they possess many of the following traits and display them frequently and with intensity:

- **Empathic:** They are attuned to the inner world of others.

- **Engaging:** They are charismatic, socially literate, and interpersonally companionable.

- **Leadership:** They can conceptualize a purpose or a vision and can formulate a direction when collaborating with others.

- **Self-possessed:** They are confident and rigorously committed to generosity and authenticity.

- **Recognition seeking:** They are fueled by positive approval and motivated to make a difference.

- **Determined:** They can push beyond dense briars of opposition.

- **Confrontational:** They hold others accountable, but without assassinating their souls.

- **Wisely fearful:** They can discern between reasonably disquieting solicitation and destructive seduction.

Conclusion

In this chapter, you've learned about the various types of narcissism, the most typical and oppressive being overt maladaptive narcissism. You've learned about the origins of narcissism and the impacts of dealing with narcissists. You've seen examples of how narcissism manifests and how it might differ by gender. You've also caught a glimpse of the implications for change and transformation. As you'll see in upcoming chapters, change is possible, but it requires innovative and courageous execution. There is a seeming conspiracy of silence that occurs between the narcissist and his authentic self, between you and your most authentic feelings when you're in his company, and between the two of you in interactions—which isn't surprising, given the often distasteful and predictable outcomes of authentic interactions between the two of you.

Moving ahead, chapter 2 takes a look at theories in psychotherapy that shed light on narcissism. It also begins to explore how these theories can be integrated to create a workable approach to the challenging emotional labyrinth we all confront when dealing with the narcissist.

chapter 2

Understanding the Anatomy of Personality: Schemas and the Brain

History, despite its wrenching pain, cannot be unlived,
but if faced with courage, need not be lived again.

—Maya Angelou

In addition to personal curiosity, over twenty years of professional experience, and exposure to a variety of talented minds in the field of human science, three leading experts have influenced my work: Aaron Beck, with his development of cognitive therapy; Jeffrey Young, creator of schema therapy; and Daniel Siegel, a trailblazer in interpersonal neurobiology. Ideas drawn from their work can serve to illuminate the way you deal with the narcissist in your life. In this chapter, I'll use the insights of these experts to take a close look at the notion of life themes and the power of natural inclinations. While the emphasis is still on understanding the narcissist, I'll also encourage you to think about your own stories and notice how the matrix of the mind and the biology of the brain can present fierce challenges. This background will help you understand what is required for growth and change in your relationship with a narcissist.

Cognitive Therapy

Aaron T. Beck, known as the father of cognitive therapy, has given countless clinicians and self-help readers a valuable compass for navigating the complex terrain of our mental and emotional belief systems. His research and clinical applications of cognitive therapy are internationally recognized, and his approach has repeatedly been proven highly effective in helping people change dysfunctional patterns of thinking and behaving. For example, as the narcissist learns to examine and accurately rescript his story of the world, along with all of its biased assumptions, he is freed from the long-standing patterns of behavior that lead to his bothersome coping behaviors, which you end up facing when in his presence.

Cognitive therapy calls for an examination of the meanings we attach to the people, places, and things in our lives. It provides, through a well-woven tapestry of concepts and strategies, a means for correcting the biased assumptions that are often connected to our negative emotional experiences and self-defeating patterns of behavior. In terms of narcissism, cognitive therapists facilitate a collaborative process by which the narcissist develops a more accurate repertoire of ideas, beliefs, and predictions, replacing the distorted thoughts that have been embedded in his mind in regard to self, others, and the future. Emphasis is placed on paying attention to self-talk and testing the reality of often biased inner dialogues. This body of work has provided fertile ground for the growth of other forms of therapy, particularly schema therapy, which has its roots in Beck's model.

Schema Therapy

Jeffrey Young is the founder of schema therapy, an integrative model of psychotherapy combining proven cognitive and behavioral techniques with other widely practiced therapies, such as interpersonal, emotion-focused, and gestalt therapy. He has made this approach accessible to the general public in books such as *Reinventing Your Life* (Young and Klosko 1994) and has further extended the reach of this powerful form of therapy through books for professionals, such as *Schema Therapy: A Practitioner's Guide* (Young, Klosko, and Weishaar 2006). Recent studies show that schema therapy offers remarkable results when used with difficult clients (Giesen-Bloo et al. 2006), and it is a superior and effective treatment approach for dealing with issues of narcissism.

Understanding Schemas

Young's schema therapy proposes eighteen early maladaptive schemas that show up in adulthood as dysfunctional life themes. They are also referred to as "buttons" or "life traps." They are considered *early* maladaptive schemas because they're derived from disquieting childhood and adolescent experiences where fundamental needs are not adequately met, which interferes with healthy and stable development. Schemas are composed of beliefs, or cognitions. They also involve emotional and bodily sensations, along with biological elements such as temperament.

Temperament refers to the innate character of the child. Along with mood, motor skills, and capacities for attention and focus, each child exhibits certain natural inclinations, such as shyness, aggression, extroversion, introversion, sensitivity, adaptability, buoyancy, and so on. These natural inclinations are shaped by genetic makeup, and they are expressed and observable in early phases of a child's development. For example, when faced with novel experiences or strangers, some very young children demonstrate an avoidant tendency and cling to their parent, caregiver, or a familiar object.

Because environmental influences can shape and modify the natural inclinations of a child, personality emerges from the interplay of the child's temperament and the environment. For example, if a shy child is constantly scorned and humiliated by a parent or caregiver, she might develop an exacerbated tendency to withdraw or, in some cases, become depressed. Paradoxically, such a child might retaliate with either aggressive acts of noncompliance or passive avoidance and detachment. A child in this situation could potentially develop a negative self-appraisal, also known as a defectiveness schema, wherein she feels flawed because she's shy.

On the other hand, if a parent shows patience and acceptance in regard to the child's discomfort and shyness, guiding her ever so gently to take small steps beyond her comfort zone, this could potentially help the child master a sense of confidence in certain novel and social situations. In this scenario, self-acceptance becomes a possibility. It is also true that temperament can change as we go through life. It isn't altogether clear what predicts lifelong versus transient temperament. But we do know that schemas are formed as a result of the interplay between a child's temperament and the difficulties she confronts in her environment.

Schemas may be dormant for much of one's life, only becoming activated by particular conditions that either mimic or challenge the unyielding beliefs embodied within them. Long held within the mind and reflecting some of the realities of the person's childhood, these "truths" become difficult to refute, in that they are the abiding content of the schema. They are often connected with painful childhood memories, discreetly sheltered within the brain, and are experienced as visceral, meaning they are sensed (but not always sensible). Because they emerge outside of awareness and therefore aren't based on present, here-and-now events, the profound and often exaggerated resonance of schemas frequently leads to self-defeating behavior patterns.

male
*
"mother"

When schemas are activated, the effects are similar to the triggering of traumatic memories. The emotional and physical circuits of the brain and body (subcortical regions) often disconnect from the executive, or decision-making, areas of the brain (cortical regions), which are responsible for distinguishing between events in the here and now versus those in the "there and then." When schemas are triggered, the resulting release of stress hormones short-circuits the executive areas of the brain, which usually allow for accuracy in reasoning and responsiveness. If you're operating from an implicit state of "there and then," your reactions and decision making can be influenced by events and emotions of the past, rather than by what's happening in the present. And worst of all, you don't even realize it because it happens behind the scenes, outside of your awareness.

So, for example, if you have a schema of abandonment due to the inextinguishably painful memory of your father's disappearance when you were six years old, you may be especially sensitive to the thought of people leaving you. When your husband tells you that he will be traveling on business, you begin to feel that insecure knot in your belly and proceed to make unreasonable demands for contact and reassurance. This sets the stage for a relationship fraught with erosive issues of mistrust and dissatisfaction.

We all have schemas, and typically more than one. They are formed in response to imperfect and sometimes traumatic early life experiences. In many cases, noxious events such as abuse, neglect, abandonment, chaos, or excessive control cause schemas to become fastened to a child's emotional makeup. This, in combination with biological predisposition, or temperament, ultimately sculpts the child's personality. When schemas are triggered by an event in the here and now ("He really pushed my buttons"), we may become flooded with uncomfortable physical sensations and biased thoughts and engage in self-defeating behaviors.

The Eighteen Early Maladaptive Schemas

In this chapter, you'll engage in a parallel process of discovery, looking at your schemas in conjunction with those of the narcissist. To begin your personal discovery, let's examine the eighteen early maladaptive schemas identified by Jeffrey Young. As you read through the material below, see if you can identify the schemas that feel true for you; also keep an eye out for schemas that may hold sway over the narcissist in your life. Keep in mind that in order for it to be a schema, it must be a feeling that first formed in your childhood or adolescence, that carries an exaggerated realness with it, and that can be intense at times, even if it is triggered only under certain conditions and is dormant most of the time. (The material below is used with the kind permission of Jeffrey Young, PhD.)

1. **Abandonment/instability.** The perceived instability or unreliability of those available for support and connection. Involves the sense that significant others will not be able to continue providing emotional support, connection, strength, or practical protection because they are emotionally unstable and unpredictable (for example, prone to angry outbursts), unreliable, or erratically present; because they will die imminently; or because they will abandon you in favor of someone better.

2. **Mistrust/abuse.** The expectation that others will hurt, abuse, humiliate, cheat, lie, manipulate, or take advantage. Usually involves the perception that the harm is intentional or the result of unjustified and extreme negligence. May include the sense that you always end up being cheated relative to others or that you are getting the short end of the stick.

deprivation. The expectation that others will not meet your desire for a normal degree of emotional ... e are three major forms of deprivation:

A. **Deprivation of nurturance:** absence of attention, affection, warmth, or companionship

B. **Deprivation of empathy:** absence of understanding, listening, self-disclosure, or mutual sharing of feelings from others

C. **Deprivation of protection:** absence of strength, direction, or guidance from others

4. **Defectiveness/shame.** The feeling that you are defective, bad, unwanted, inferior, or invalid in important respects or that you would be unlovable to significant others if exposed. May involve hypersensitivity to criticism, rejection, and blame; self-consciousness, comparisons, and insecurity around others; or a sense of shame regarding your perceived flaws. These flaws may be private (for example, selfishness, angry impulses, or unacceptable sexual desires) or public (such as undesirable physical appearance or social awkwardness).

5. **Social isolation/alienation.** The feeling that you are isolated from the rest of the world, different from other people, and/or not part of any group or community.

6. **Dependence/incompetence.** The belief that you are unable to handle everyday responsibilities in a competent manner without considerable help from others (for example, take care of yourself, solve daily problems, exercise good judgment, tackle new tasks, or make good decisions). Often feels like helplessness.

7. **Vulnerability to harm or illness.** Exaggerated fear that imminent catastrophe will strike at any time and that you will be unable to prevent it. Fears focus on one or more of the following: medical catastrophes, such as heart attacks or AIDS; emotional catastrophes, such as "going crazy"; or external catastrophes, such as

elevators collapsing, being victimized by criminals, airplane crashes, or earthquakes.

8. **Enmeshment/undeveloped self.** Excessive emotional involvement and closeness with one or more significant others (often parents) at the expense of your individual identity or normal social development. Often involves the belief that you cannot survive or be happy without the constant support of the enmeshed other. May also include feelings of being smothered by or fused with others. You may feel a lack of sufficient individual identity. Often experienced as a feeling of emptiness and floundering, having no direction, or, in extreme cases, questioning your existence.

9. **Failure.** The belief that you have failed, will inevitably fail, or are fundamentally inadequate relative to your peers in areas of achievement (such as school, career, or sports). Often involves beliefs that you are stupid, inept, untalented, ignorant, lower in status, less successful than others, and so on.

10. **Entitlement/grandiosity.** The belief that you are superior to other people, entitled to special rights and privileges, or not bound by the rules of reciprocity that guide normal social interaction. Often involves insistence that you should be able to do or have whatever you want, regardless of what is realistic, what others consider reasonable, or the cost to others. Also common is an exaggerated focus on superiority (for example, being among the most successful, famous, wealthy) in order to achieve power or control (not primarily for attention or approval). Sometimes includes excessive competitiveness toward or domination of others: asserting your power, forcing your point of view, or controlling the behavior of others in line with your own desires—without empathy or concern for others' needs or feelings.

11. **Insufficient self-control/self-discipline.** Pervasive difficulty or refusal to exercise sufficient self-control and tolerate frustration to achieve your personal goals, or to restrain the excessive expression

of your emotions and impulses. In its milder form, you may experience a tendency to avoid discomfort: avoiding pain, conflict, confrontation, responsibility, or overexertion—at the expense of personal fulfillment, commitment, or integrity.

12. Subjugation. Excessive surrendering of control to others because you feel coerced—usually to avoid anger, retaliation, or abandonment. There are two major forms of subjugation:

√A. **Subjugation of needs:** suppression of your preferences, decisions, and desires

√B. **Subjugation of emotions:** suppression of emotional expression, especially anger

Usually involves the perception that your desires, opinions, and feelings are not valid or important to others. Frequently, there is a tendency toward excessive compliance combined with hypersensitivity to feeling trapped. Generally leads to a buildup of anger, which can lead to passive-aggressive behavior, uncontrolled outbursts of temper, psychosomatic symptoms, withdrawal of affection, acting out, and substance abuse.

13. Self-sacrifice. Excessive focus on voluntarily meeting the needs of others in daily situations at the expense of your own gratification. The most common reasons are to prevent causing pain to others, to avoid guilt from feeling selfish, or to maintain the connection with others perceived as needy. Often results from an acute sensitivity to the pain of others. Sometimes leads to a sense that your own needs are not being adequately met and to resentment of those who are taken care of. (Overlaps with the concept of codependency.)

14. Approval seeking/recognition seeking. Excessive emphasis on gaining approval, recognition, or attention from other people, or fitting in, at the expense of developing a secure and true sense of self. Your sense of self-esteem is dependent primarily on the reactions of others rather than on your own natural inclinations. Sometimes includes an overemphasis on status, appearance, social acceptance, money, or achievement—as means of gaining approval, admiration, or attention (not primarily for power or control). Frequently results in major life decisions that are inauthentic or unsatisfying, or in hypersensitivity to rejection.

15. Negativity/pessimism. A pervasive, lifelong focus on the negative aspects of life (pain, death, loss, disappointment, conflict, guilt, resentment, unsolved problems, potential mistakes, betrayal, things that could go wrong, and so on) while minimizing or neglecting the positive or optimistic aspects. Usually includes an exaggerated expectation—in a wide range of work, financial, or interpersonal situations—that things will eventually go seriously wrong, or that aspects of your life that seem to be going well will ultimately fall apart. Usually involves an inordinate fear of making mistakes that might lead to financial collapse, loss, humiliation, or being trapped in a bad situation. Because potential negative outcomes are exaggerated, chronic worry, vigilance, complaining, or indecision frequently characterize your behaviors.

16. Emotional inhibition. The excessive inhibition of spontaneous action, feeling, or communication—usually to avoid disapproval by others, feelings of shame, or losing control of your impulses. The most common areas of inhibition involve inhibition of anger and aggression; inhibition of positive impulses (such as joy, affection, sexual excitement, or play); difficulty expressing vulnerability or communicating freely about your feelings, needs, and so on; and excessive emphasis on rational wisdom while disregarding emotions.

17. Unrelenting standards/hypercriticalness. The underlying belief that you must strive to meet very high internalized standards of behavior and performance, usually to avoid criticism. Typically results in feelings of pressure or difficulty slowing down, and in hypercriticalness toward yourself and others. Involves a significant impairment in pleasure, relaxation, health, self-esteem, sense of accomplishment, or satisfying relationships. Unrelenting standards typically appear in three forms:

A. **Perfectionism**, inordinate attention to detail, or an underestimate of how good your performance is relative to the norm

B. **Rigid rules and "shoulds"** in many areas of life, including unrealistically high moral, ethical, cultural, or religious precepts

C. **Preoccupation with time and efficiency**, so that more can be accomplished

18. **Punitiveness.** The belief that people should be harshly punished for making mistakes. Involves the tendency to be angry, intolerant, punitive, and impatient with those people (including yourself) who do not meet your expectations or standards. Usually includes difficulty forgiving mistakes in yourself or others because of a reluctance to consider extenuating circumstances, allow for human imperfection, or empathize with feelings.

Jeffrey Young, PhD. Unauthorized reproduction without the written consent of the author is prohibited.

Using Schemas to Understand Interactions with a Narcissist

You might find that you and the narcissist in your life have, within your collections, some matching schemas, which may have originated from either similar or very different backgrounds. What differentiates the two of you, despite those potentially similar schemas, is the way in which you cope with them. Let's say, for example, that you grew up with a mom who was very subjugated and self-sacrificing—not just giving and generous, but truly with little capacity to express her own needs and wants. She may have been a "path of least resistance" type of person who avoided confrontations and felt guilty when she was the center of attention. She may have occasionally shown signs of resentment when she was tired and overburdened by her load or if she felt stifled about something important to her. You may have adopted this schema as a result of witnessing her ways with people, including the unruly ones. As a result, you may tend to enact your self-sacrificing and subjugation schemas by giving in whenever the narcissist in your life activates the "play" button on your internal tape. This type of response is particularly characteristic of women.

Unfortunately, this coping style will perpetuate the very schemas you seek to escape. The more you give in to your self-sacrificing and subjugation beliefs, perhaps by enabling the narcissist's bad habits or keeping your mouth shut as requested, the more strength these beliefs will gain in keeping you stuck. It's not your fault, however. It's an automatic process that, without awareness, understanding, and hard work, will continue to show up, just like the sun rising each day in the eastern sky.

The following list of schemas typically triggered by interactions with a narcissist will help you see that when you surrender or give in as a means of coping, you are actually blocking effective healing of schema-driven beliefs and behaviors that hold your assertive voice hostage.

Typical Schemas That Get Triggered by Narcissists

- **Self-sacrifice:** It's tough to ask for what you need without feeling unworthy or guilty. Narcissists make it even tougher. You can get torn between feelings of guilt and resentment.

- **Subjugation:** It's difficult to be assertive when it comes to your personal rights and opinions. Narcissists can be intimidating, forcing you to bury your anger or denying you your point of view.

- **Abandonment/instability:** Because you are so fearful of being rejected or alone, you will put up with the limitations and tormenting behaviors of your narcissist.

- **Defectiveness/shame:** Because you feel inadequate and undesirable, you easily buy into the criticisms that are hurled at you by the narcissist, taking the blame and feeling it's your fault when he's unhappy with you. You often feel that you need to fix yourself.

- **Emotional inhibition:** With this schema, you are in the habit of keeping your feelings to yourself and are stoic and overly controlled when it comes to your emotions. The narcissist can have emotional outbursts, while you stand by in silent, invisible sorrow.

- **Emotional deprivation:** With this schema, you don't believe that you can find someone to meet your emotional needs, to really love you and understand you, to protect you and care about you. The narcissist lives up to your expectation. You are sad, but this is familiar.

- **Mistrust/abuse:** With this schema, your relationship with the narcissist when he's in his hurtful or abusive mode feels like a reenactment of the past. You know how to put up with it, and it feels impossible to fight it. Even when you try to fight, you usually end up giving in.

- **Unrelenting standards:** With this schema, you try harder and harder to be the perfect partner, friend, sibling, or employee, because you believe that this is expected of you. You compromise pleasure and spontaneity in an effort to live up to the narcissist's standards.

Now, as you read the following list of schemas typical of narcissists, note how the narcissist tries to fight his schemas or overcompensate for them. He avoids contacting the emotions associated with his schemas rather than surrendering to them.

Typical Schemas Associated with Narcissism

- **Emotional deprivation:** No one will ever meet his needs and love him for who he is. Therefore, he must never need anyone. He strives for perfection, success, and autonomy.

- **Mistrust/abuse:** He believes that people are nice to him only because they want something from him. He avoids true intimacy and is highly skeptical of the motives of others.

- **Defectiveness/shame:** At a very core, unaware level, he feels unlovable and ashamed of himself. He keeps that realization away from his consciousness by indulging in addictive self-soothing activities (including workaholism), demanding approval for his outstanding performance, and acting entitled to special treatment.

- **Subjugation:** Control or be controlled. He is controlling.

- **Unrelenting standards:** There's no time for spontaneity, which can be a threat to his well-masked sense of inadequacy. He must sacrifice pleasure in order to do things perfectly, and often relentlessly. He's restless when out of his performance mode.

- **Entitlement/grandiosity:** This is the narcissist's hallmark schema. He feels special when he's treated differently than other people. The rules don't apply to him. He has grandiose dreams and a sense of supreme self-importance. This is also a cover-up for a sense of defectiveness.

- **Insufficient self-control:** He refuses to accept limits and has little tolerance for discomfort. The narcissist wants what he wants, in whatever quantity or time frame he chooses, and cannot tolerate having to wait or being refused what he wants.

- **Approval seeking:** His is a constant search for recognition, status, and the attention of others. This is usually an over-compensation for his loneliness and sense of defectiveness.

Origins of the Narcissist's Schemas

Schemas correlated with the narcissist frequently arise in a scenario like this: Picture a child who grew up in a home where he was routinely criticized and devalued—where he was made to feel unworthy of love and attention, and where he ultimately developed a defectiveness/shame schema. He also contracted the emotional deprivation schema because his caregivers didn't show him much affection, understanding, or protection. His mistrust and subjugation schemas were derived from feeling controlled and manipulated by parents who expected him to take care of their self-esteem by adhering to their standards for performance and surrendering his own important childhood needs. With no significant adult to counterbalance this experience and no repair work done by his depriving, critical parents, he grew up with an undercurrent of loneliness and shame, along with a well-entrenched feeling that no one would ever meet his emotional needs and that he was unlovable and flawed. These are the endlessly repeated lyrics of his schema, the biased beliefs that he has rigidly internalized.

During childhood, the repetitive and painful feelings linked to these experiences soon became file folders within his brain—file folders harboring the intractable "truths" that will define him, his future, and the world around him. His schemas acted as a blueprint for his emotional architecture. By early adulthood, the simple act of entering a room full of strangers becomes a schema-triggering experience; he opens up the file folder and, based on the information within, anticipates being judged, ignored, or rejected by others.

As a child, he sought to escape the pain associated with his environment, establishing coping skills that disabled healthy interpersonal connectedness but enabled him to thrive amid the voids and ruptures. Those coping skills often involve donning three protective masks:

- **The perfectionist:** the hallmark of an unrelenting standards schema

- **The avenging bully:** the hallmark of an entitlement schema

- **The competitive braggart:** the hallmark of an approval-seeking schema

Coping Responses in Schema Theory

As part of our human nature, our brains are wired to respond to a threat of danger through the fight-or-flight response. Actually, that's a misnomer, as the response can manifest in three different ways: You can fight, or counterattack. You can flee, running from the danger or otherwise avoiding it. Or you can freeze, giving in or surrendering to the threat. When a schema is triggered, it can produce a sense of threat due to the extremely powerful negative emotions, thoughts, physical sensations, and self-defeating reactions that arise out of early maladaptive experiences. Present-day circumstances that mirror the memories embedded in the schema will send a resonant message to the brain and body. The brain responds to the perceived threat by attempting to fight the schema, flee the schema, or surrender to the schema. All three responses are mechanisms for keeping the schema from getting its mighty grip on us. The battle with the internal phantom becomes a quagmire. As explained above, schemas are typically triggered without the person being aware of what is happening behind the scenes. You are often only aware of the feeling of a present danger or imminent threat based on a suggestive stimulus.

For example, let's say your supervisor walks by your desk with a seemingly unusual look on her face. If you have a defectiveness, abandonment, or mistrust schema, you may be prone to jumping to conclusions or predicting loss and rejection whenever you perceive someone to be unhappy with you. As a result, you're likely to feel that your supervisor is upset with you and instantly experience a knot in your stomach, a pounding heart, and a voice in your head that says, *That's it; I'm fired.* Even if you have a keen facility for reasonable thinking and testing reality and can produce no evidence to make the case that you're being fired, you'll still feel queasy and unable to abort this feeling of dread, because beneath the surface of rational explanation lies the schema. Like an infection, the schema doesn't respond to the first round of practical interventions. You may ultimately—and frequently—find your negative expectations unwarranted but still be unable to halt the careening process once a schema is triggered. You may even recognize it as a familiar unease, reminiscent of something but without definitive clarity as to its origins.

Our brains are primed to launch protective missiles when an enemy is present, and in this case the schema is the enemy. Ironically, in an effort to seek refuge from this predator, we often end up right back in its grip. Again, let's consider the scenario of that "funny look" on your supervisor's face: If your particular potion for eradicating this worrisome sense of doom is to flee to safety, you might find yourself avoiding tasks, becoming preoccupied and distracted, making mistakes, engaging in gloomy dialogues with colleagues, and ultimately actually putting yourself at risk. You could end up the recipient of a disciplinary action for a decline in performance, having shifted into an avoidant and distracted coping mode. If you have an abandonment schema—one that predicts an exaggerated number of losses and rejections—you may, despite your attempts to dodge it, end up chanting the old familiar verses of the schema. (Recall the example of the woman with the abandonment schema whose husband had to travel for business. Her fears led to unreasonable and relentless demands for contact and reassurance, which could ultimately damage the relationship, priming the possibility of yet another loss.)

In the extreme case, if your fears and your adoption of protective measures become chronic patterns in the workplace, you might actually end up getting fired. Self-fulfilling prophecy? No. Ironic? No. Guided by implicit impulses, you are a creature of habit, unknowingly navigating toward the familiar, even those very painful familiar feelings you seek to avoid. You need to stop dodging the bullets unless you determine that they are indeed bullets. But stopping your habitual behavior will feel counterintuitive.

We are all primed for survival, but we aren't always clear on what represents a genuine threat to survival. The challenge of dealing with a narcissist can abduct your sense of discernment, leaving you feeling like you're forever facing the threat of a charging grizzly bear or sentenced to inhabit the barren aloneness of a dark cave. The goal is to distinguish genuine threats from schemas that distort your perceptions and responses. To do this, you need to make the implicit more explicit; you need to become aware of inner motivations in a way that is felt, not just understood. Chapter 5 will provide detailed exercises that utilize mindfulness strategies to help you differentiate threat from challenge and harness a felt sense of your motivational engines, which drive your response patterns.

• *Louis's Story*

Louis, a fifty-eight-year-old man, provides a good example of the self-perpetuating dilemmas a narcissist faces. One of Louis's schemas is defectiveness/shame. Due to his childhood experiences, Louis developed a deeply held (though not explicitly conscious) feeling that he was inadequate and unlovable. He and his wife, Francine, have been married for thirty-two years. They have two grown sons, both married and living in other parts of the country. About two years ago, Louis retired from a Fortune 100 company. A highly successful man, he is widely recognized and respected in his field, and he's attained impressive financial security. Francine is a schoolteacher who continues to enjoy her work and has no desire to retire anytime soon.

Francine came to see me in the hopes that I might be willing to work with Louis and perhaps with the two of them together at some point. It was evident that Francine had become fairly sturdy in her compassionate understanding of Louis, thanks to her own time in therapy and various self-help efforts. These experiences had also deepened her self-awareness and helped her develop greater skills for asserting herself. Feeling more equipped, she'd been able to confront Louis on more than thirty years of critical, self-absorbed, avoidant, and obnoxious behavior. She was also able to identify her own chronic issues of compliance and passivity in her relationship with Louis, as well as others.

Unfortunately, despite her candor and devotion, nothing was changing. She had begun to prepare herself for the possibility of separation if Louis wouldn't consent to some form of therapy and finally gave him an ultimatum. Louis was no stranger to therapy. He had "visited" therapists many times before. It was always short-lived, as Francine would minimize her complaints or Louis would mow down the therapist with his unyielding sarcasm and intimidation. But Francine had made it clear to Louis that if things didn't change this time, she would leave him. Having heard that I was an expert in high-conflict relationships and narcissism, Francine saw this as their one last chance—no pressure, of course—to save their marriage.

Louis is an attractive man, well dressed right down to his countless pairs of expensive loafers. Intelligent and well educated, he proudly mentions his abundant library of classic literature. He enjoys name-dropping. Louis plays tennis four times a week and golf on the other days. When off the courts and the course, he is mostly engaged in solitary activities like reading, surfing the Web, or managing his investment portfolio. His few friends are mostly through Francine. Even his tennis and golf mates are former business acquaintances whom he has little personal attachment to, other than competing in sports, talking about investments, or quibbling about politics. His sons call him, but mainly for business advice and for loans. He misses them.

Louis would like Francine to retire so they could travel more. He is adamantly disinterested in her enthusiasm for her work. He is insulting and puts her down, admonishing her "simple" profession. But now Louis is worried and agitated because Francine has threatened to leave him and she seems serious. For the first time, there is leverage for change.

Leverage and Incentive

Leverage comes in many forms: for example, a potential or actual significant loss (such as a loved one's threat to leave), a disabling medical condition, retirement, termination of a job, financial instability, legal challenges, or sometimes the unstoppable ache of loneliness or depression (which may come with persistent isolation) or the mellowing passage of time. With leverage, the possibility for insight and change emerges. Incentive also helps, though it isn't as easy to cultivate. To the narcissist, the possibility of achieving shame-free and secure connections, a sense of belonging, and liberation from the burden of having to constantly prove his self-worth probably sounds good. But because he has no prior experience to draw upon and plenty of success in the world of excessive autonomy, these incentives are likely to seem unattainable and even unimaginable. I often find myself telling my narcissistic clients that they aren't changing because they either aren't in enough pain yet or don't have anything tangible enough to reach for, apart from

TROUTBECK

their unrelenting desire for fame and glory. This had been the case for Louis throughout his entire marriage, but now, for the first time in his adult life, he was experiencing enough pain and fear that change could potentially occur.

Louis's Schemas in Action

Louis's schemas are easily triggered in social settings, such as when he's on the golf course with Jack, a former business colleague. In an effort to not feel shameful and rejected, Louis postures himself in his approval-seeking mode, where he aggrandizes himself with incessant talk about his rank and standing at the club. At first, Jack may be amused or impressed by the content and gallant style of Louis's speech. But inevitably he grows tired, annoyed, and put off, and eventually he ends up thinking, *Who does he think he is? What a self-centered bore. Somebody get me out of here!* Louis, in the mighty grip of his defectiveness/shame schema, has inspired the very thing he was trying to avoid: rejection and disapproval. The inner stirrings of the schema and the automatic decision to hide it through show-off behaviors simply perpetuate it.

So, you might ask, is Louis simply a masochist, or are all humans hopelessly at the mercy of habitual beliefs about the world and their rank within it? Neither. In order to grasp the power and possibility of change, we need to take a close look at the elegant and intricately assembled apparatus of the brain and how it relates to both nature (genetic precursors like temperament) and nurture (the security or lack thereof within the parent-child relationship).

Foundations of Security: Biology and Attachment

Daniel J. Siegel, a child psychiatrist and expert in family dynamics, as well as a leader in the development of interpersonal neurobiology, proposes that childhood attachment experiences directly influence emotions, behavior, autobiographical memory, and one's personal narrative. He's written several influential books addressing these topics, including *The Developing Mind* (2001), *Parenting from the Inside Out* (Siegel and Hartzell 2004), and *The Mindful Brain* (2007). Although Siegel's focus isn't on narcissists, his theories shed a great deal of light on this personality type.

Attachment and the Brain

Siegel's work is informed by a thoughtful examination of theories of attachment, neurobiology, parent-child relationships, and mindful awareness, along with a compelling look at the mind, relationships, and the brain. His discoveries in interpersonal neurobiology offer an innovative guidepost for those who are trying to make sense out of their biased and sometimes dysfunctional reactions to the world, and who are seeking evidence for the possibility of personal growth and change. Siegel's works offer an enlightening and accessible tutorial on the intricate assemblage of our most profound personal labyrinth: the brain. Like Jeffrey Young, he points the needle of the compass toward an assessment of the level of security in the parent-child relationship, combined with the native capacities of the child.

Siegel also helps us appreciate how the brain, with its infinite number of functions and extraordinary depth, has the power to connect us with memory-driven states of mind in a matter of seconds. For example, you might find yourself drifting back to a loving and nostalgic memory of your grandma and her delicious apple pies as you encounter a similar wondrous aroma wafting out of the bakery on your way to the office. The mind also has the power to retrieve the sadness linked with a tucked-away memory of rejection. For example, maybe you're unconsciously recalling your father, who was too busy to notice your longing to be hugged, when you find yourself gripped by a sudden melancholic twinge while sitting in a restaurant on a Saturday night, trying to capture your spouse's attention as he peruses the menu and scans his electronic organizer.

You know the feeling: Perhaps you're driving along and a song comes on the radio that suddenly transports you to another time and place, maybe a first love or a first loss. Your body becomes filled with sensations and heightened awareness. You don't always immediately know why you are feeling that way. It may take a while to pluck the memory from your archives. But your brain is way ahead of your mind, making connections to what might sound like, taste like, smell like, look like, or feel like something you've experienced before. It is the grand master of association and meaning, but it isn't always correct in its assessment of a person, place, or thing. It's kind of like the old game Concentration, where you lay picture cards face down and then turn them over two at a time, trying to find a matched pair. Your brain is primed to probe its memory files in search of that which has been experienced, observed, and stored. It is the library of your personal experience.

When you access memory, you access your resources for imagination, intuition, learning, and logical thinking. Your internal environment is both stable and ever changing. Because of memory, you are capable of adapting, learning new things, and attaching meaning to your experiences. In its quest for familiarity and stability, your brain constantly asks the question *What does that mean?*— though this often occurs below the radar of your awareness. It is memory that offers assistance as you drive a familiar route, allowing you to listen to the radio, sip your coffee, and hardly pay attention to the rights and the lefts. You know the way; it is automatically summoned from your reference file.

However, should you happen to come across the dreaded detour sign, you will put down your coffee, lower the volume of the radio, and sharpen your focus. This is an example of your brain on a mission of seeking the familiar and predictable. Suddenly, with your attention fully engaged and deliberately focused on the moment, you look ahead for those anticipated orange signs that point you toward a recognizable landmark, putting you back on track. You breathe easier when you figure it out. We are all pleasure seekers relying on the power of the brain (which is primed to avoid pain) to help us find our way out of uncomfortable situations.

So what does this have to do with narcissism? The learned experiences of your lifetime, along with your innate drive, tendencies, and idiosyncratic makeup, are filed in many categorical memory folders in your brain. Among the folders one is titled "How I get to work each day," and another is "How I feel and what I do when I'm with an obnoxious person who needs constant admiration, makes me feel small or invisible, and has to be right about everything." So when you encounter Mr. Charming in the office on Monday, your expectations and reactions are predetermined by the content of that memory folder. You might, however, actively engage your brain in seeking out a different route.

One client told me that in AA meetings there is a saying that goes something like this: The definition of insanity is doing the exact same thing over and over again and expecting a different result. No, you're not insane. But it sometimes feels that way when nothing changes despite your tenacious efforts. Harnessing a keen awareness of your present moment and trying a new approach can feel awkward and unnatural, given your past experiences. If you know yourself to be a people pleaser and a person who never rocks the boat, this makes it difficult to imagine taking a different approach. The history of your experience is powerful and can dominate your reactions, but it isn't necessarily relevant to the here and now. So, just because someone once intimidated you into believing that you had nothing important to say and that you should keep quiet and maintain peace at all costs, that doesn't mean it's true now. It wasn't true then either, but as a child, your ability to forge your own beliefs and choose your responses was limited. You may have done the best you could as a child, but you can make new choices as an adult.

Creatures of Habit

As part of the human condition, we are essentially guided by memories, both explicit (the ones we vividly recall) and implicit (the ones we remember without knowing we're remembering them). This concept validates the ideas that Jeffrey Young proposes in schema theory and allows us to probe where life themes reside within the brain—in explicit or implicit memory. As it turns out, our schemas, or personal life themes, often wind up in the implicit storage container, outside of our awareness. When they're triggered, we may become aware of bodily, emotional, and cognitive changes without having a clear perception of the memories that evoked those changes, and perhaps without even understanding that memories are responsible for those changes. This causes us to feel childlike and powerless, igniting the well-designed mechanics of moving from threat to safety.

Living in a triggered state is like living in a "once upon a time" place where sensory reenactments of an early experience eclipse the present moment. When feeling at risk or sensing a threat, we usually turn to familiar strategies to banish our demons, soothe the soul, and recast our appearance to the world. Within the wardrobe of your brain, you have many vintage costumes to outfit your states of mind and camouflage your discomfort. When threatened, some of us become transformed into vengeful warriors, some into do-gooders or self-righteous preachers, and yet others into perilous perfectionists or unstoppable intellectualizers. At times, we also show up as healthy grown-up folks with rational reactions grounded in the here and now.

•   *Young Louis: The Burgeoning Narcissist*

Louis, discussed earlier in this chapter, grew up with a critical and demanding father and a socially preoccupied mother. The oldest of four children, he was the one who became a companion to his mom during his dad's extended business travels and long workdays. Louis was smart and a very good athlete, and he received a great deal of praise and attention for his achievements. Because he was the oldest, and because his mother was so distracted, Louis had few limits placed upon him. He was raised to believe that he was special and that any problems were "the other guy's fault."

His dad made it known that no son of his would dare embarrass him with less-than-perfect grades or a less-than-perfect performance in any public setting. His dad also made it quite clear that any expression of fear or sadness was a sign of weakness. So Louis courageously endured countless nights of sitting alone at home, studying or practicing his clarinet—which he hated—while his parents took the younger children out for ice cream or other special treats. Louis was constantly told that he was bound for great things; he was special. Loneliness became a familiar state for him, whether he was alone or among others. He had poor interpersonal skills—not surprising given that his primary role models were myopically focused on achievement and self-control. Within his family, he had no examples of empathy or emotional connectedness to others.

As an adolescent, Louis was awkward with girls. And because of his all-too-familiar feeling of shame, masked by a bellowing "Who cares; no one's worth my time, anyway" attitude, he distracted himself with academic competitiveness and solitary activities, including indulging in grandiose fantasies of fame and fortune. Before long, Louis's maladaptive schemas, which included emotional deprivation, defectiveness/shame, mistrust, entitlement, and approval seeking, became the wallpaper of his internal life.

Connecting the Dots

Louis, like many others with these issues, was determined to create a life that would afford him enough self-sufficiency to shelter him from the longings and loneliness of his past. But the brain is an unyielding concierge that insists on ringing in with wake-up calls despite the desire to remain in peaceful slumber, free from the responsibility of attending to the undernourished soul. Human beings are wired for love and connection to others, and the brain will strive to achieve these goals despite the roadblocks schemas present.

Researchers in the field of parent-child attachment provide much data to support this truth. And so it is with Louis, who repeatedly hits the snooze button on his internal wake-up call and instead moves aggressively through life disguised in his impeccably starched veneer. He racks up his extraordinary references, displays magnanimous goals, and indulges in solitary soothing all in the service of not feeling the "shameful little weakling" held hostage beneath his skin. His impatience with "lesser mortals" and "small talk" leaves him barely able to notice the impact of his boorish behavior on others who might love him and long to be loved by him. Louis moves in a world of extraordinariness where any experience of being ordinary or being surrounded by ordinary people, places, and events is the equivalent of being emotionally helpless, needy, defective, and unworthy. The demand to don the cloak of uniqueness and superiority, once externally driven by the needs and demands of his parents, has become entirely internalized and self-imposed.

Conclusion

In combination with biological makeup, early experience can dramatically shape our impressions, beliefs, and responses vis-à-vis the world we live in. Given that we are creatures of habit who gravitate toward the familiar, it makes sense that early maladaptive schemas can be like a boomerang, often leading us back to where we started despite our efforts to move away from that place. Understanding the finely honed mechanisms of the brain gives us an appreciation for how cumbersome change is, while also affirming that change is possible. For all of us, grasping and accepting the anatomical realities of memory and its associational tendencies can help mediate obstacles to change, like shame and self-blame.

If the narcissist in your life is amenable to seeking professional help, look for a therapist who can be empathically confrontational. In a limited but necessary way, the therapist must reparent the wounded side of the narcissist. If you choose to seek professional assistance for yourself, the therapist should be able to escort you to an excavation of your own schemas and idiosyncratic obstacles to healthy assertiveness. Your therapist must help bolster you against reluctance or resignation so that you can make healthy and wise choices for yourself when dealing with the narcissist. In my experience, this approach loosens the clutch of a long-standing sense of shame and hopelessness—not just for you, but also for the narcissist. Your authentic self can emerge, grounded in wisdom, empathy, and self-advocacy, and the narcissist can become connected, receptive, and responsible. This approach enhances the possibility for healing the hurt and engaging the lonely and precious exiled parts of both of you.

chapter 3

Getting Captured: Identifying Your Personal Traps

And since you know you cannot see yourself,
so well as by reflection, I, your glass,
will modestly discover to yourself,
that of yourself which you yet know not of.

—William Shakespeare

Now that you've sharpened your understanding of the origins of narcissism, the ways it manifests, and schemas related to narcissism, let's point the lens toward you, the person on the receiving end of the relationship. When under the narcissist's spell, you may not be able to clearly see what is happening inside your mind and body. You may feel ineffective and unsatisfied with your ways of dealing with this trying person. You're not alone in finding it difficult to interact with a narcissist. In my practice, clients in similar situations repeatedly ask certain questions:

- What's with me? Am I simply a masochist?

- How can I allow myself to be so fooled?

- Why am I so drawn to these difficult people?

- Am I being punished?

- How do these trying people always find me?

- Do I have "doormat" written on my forehead?

- Why can't I just speak up and tell him to…

It can be difficult to assess toxic interactions during the early phase of any relationship, particularly if you're only in the narcissist's presence from time to time. Even when it seems apparent that he is a bit obnoxious, you may have grown up with the message *Too bad; just deal with it* implanted in your brain, especially if the narcissist in your life happens to be an authority figure, such as a boss, supervisor, or professor, or even a romantic partner. You aren't foolish, nor are you being punished, and you definitely don't have a self-defeating label emblazoned on your brow. The narcissist's charm and wit can be very hypnotizing, encouraging you to be forgiving when he's out of line. You're drawn to this person because he is attractive in some ways. It can be difficult to speak up. The costs may appear too great, and if you've been in the relationship for a while, you've been well trained in the art of diplomacy—or, rather, biting your tongue.

Comfort Zones: The Challenges of Living with and Changing Your Habits

Despite the well-worn soles, poor support, and unsightly appearance of our comfortable old shoes, we choose to keep them because they have come to fit us well, customized by the memory of the movement of the heel, the instep, and each toe. We feel we can endure long walks in these shoes because of their familiar fit. This is also the case with our relationships and our styles of relating with others. When faced with a difficult situation, you're likely to rely on what you know—the automatic patterns programmed into your brain's response system. It's only when the "heel comes loose" in a relationship, or the pain becomes too great, that we begin to experience depression, anxiety, and stress. Once things become this painful, you may be willing to break out of your comfort zone and repair those old shoes, or maybe toss them out and try something new, even if it's uncomfortable at first.

Your early experience of the world—from navigating the continent of your crib with visitors' faces looming above you to scaling the slope of your mother's lap in search of comfort to negotiating the playground in search of recognition and inclusion—provided many thoughts and sensations that you have collected and stored in your memory library for future reference. Retrieval of these souvenirs, such as what might happen when you cry, laugh, or show fear or anger, and what to do about it, requires little effort given the repetitious nature of so much of our experience and how predictable the outcomes often are. From our early years as helpless little beings, we are informed by the distress of travels fraught with countless letdowns and emotional compromises, but in the process we become equipped with a compass for survival.

We learn quickly what we can expect from the world, from the people in it, and from ourselves. The well-designed architectural landscape of the brain is expansive, providing space for thoughts, feelings, behaviors, and bodily sensations. It encompasses countless rooms for our inhabitance. Experience is the concierge of the mind, discreetly guiding us from room to room.

Why the Narcissist Triggers You

Take a few moments to look back at the eighteen schemas described in chapter 2 and once again identify your schemas. If you're like most people, you'll find that several of the schemas seem to fit. It's very common for schemas to occur in clusters. Some of the groupings most common among people in relationships with narcissists are mistrust and subjugation; defectiveness and unrelenting standards; and abandonment, emotional deprivation, and self-sacrifice. Let's take a closer look at those three clusters.

Mistrust and Subjugation

You might find yourself identifying with the mistrust and subjugation schemas if your internal autobiography tells the story of a child who was taken advantage of or mistreated. As such, your reaction to manipulative or abusive people is to subjugate yourself by tucking in your feelings and doing what you're told to do. If you had no one to protect you when you were a child, this may have been the only reasonable way to survive. Now that you're an adult, when the narcissist in your life becomes controlling or demanding or puts you down with criticism and blame, your old memories are fired up (beneath your actual awareness), along with habitual reactions.

Your protective mechanisms cause you to respond to the control and abuse by shutting down and doing what you're told to do. However, there's a problem with your inner sentry system: the long-choreographed movements are in dire need of a tune-up or overhaul. Anchored in the past, your habitual beliefs and responses are outdated, yet they capture you and hold you hostage. As a result, you lose your voice and forfeit your rights.

Defectiveness and Unrelenting Standards

If you have a combination of the defectiveness and unrelenting standards schemas, this might be because you were made to feel unlovable, inadequate, or flawed as a child. In response, you may have made your best effort to be good and acceptable and to get it right in order to avoid criticism, achieve acceptance, and enjoy loving attention.

In the here and now, when the narcissist in your life is critical or withholding, you work as hard as you can to be the perfect friend, spouse, coworker, or sibling. Unfortunately, you're dancing to a distant drummer within an orchestra of memories playing outdated tunes.

Abandonment, Emotional Deprivation, and Self-Sacrifice

You may have a combination of abandonment, emotional deprivation, and self-sacrifice schemas if you grew up feeling that there was no one you could truly count on, that the people you loved could leave you, or that they would never truly understand you or give you the love, affection, and support you needed. You may have arrived at these beliefs due to the instability of an alcoholic parent, the loss of a caregiver, a divorce, or perhaps a parent who was too depressed to nurture you adequately.

Through a combination of temperament and experience, you may have put your needs aside to focus on taking care of others. If you felt like a burden to your parents and were sensitive to their upsets and expectations, you probably worked hard to please them (and others), asking for little in return and enjoying whatever crumbs came your way. Any resentment about being deprived or abandoned was eclipsed by an ever-presiding sense of guilt.

As a result, when dealing with the narcissist in your life you carefully walk the narrow, eggshell-lined path, keeping your own needs tucked away. Fearful of losing him or igniting his short fuse, you give in, enabling him and sacrificing your own needs. That is, of course, until your wise and hungry mind tunes in, filling you with resentment and launching you into your own "what about me" tirade. Unfortunately, this just sets you up for his fiery reaction to the hurts and longings you dared to voice, and—ta-da!—you return to your familiar post of guilt-ridden giver.

Developing an Authentic Voice

Of course, it may be that when you find yourself tested or triggered by difficult interactions with you know who, you fight back by bullying, demanding, or threatening. And while you appear to possess a formidable voice, the primary opponent in your battle is only a phantom: the enemy emerging from your memory's archives. You feel your buttons getting pushed, and you counterattack or get defensive. However, there is a difference between taking a stand for yourself—utilizing an authentic and assertive voice against abuse, control, and oppression—and defending yourself with contempt, criticalness, and self-righteousness.

Let's go back to the case of Louis, from chapter 2, for a moment. As he launches one of his usual degrading assaults on his wife, Francine, she hears his harsh and uncaring sentiments and feels her emotional deprivation and self-sacrifice schemas getting fired up. However, she feels this indirectly, in the form of tenseness in her jaw, queasiness in her gut, and heat rising into her face. She hears her inner voice saying, *I am sick of forever doing and giving but getting nothing back in return. I've never gotten my needs met, and I never will. I've had it!* And so Francine, now sturdy with her righteous anger, attempts to fight back, loudly declaring, "I've been a good wife. I've tried to do my best, but you never appreciate anything. You're inhuman; you're the one who's a loser." She exits the living room, slams the door, and heads for the bedroom, where she will cry alone yet again. At first glance, we may cheer for her as she courageously takes on her inimitable partner: "You go, girl!"

However, as the scene continues to unfold, Louis's stunned reaction becomes a shrug and a smirk. If you could enter the domain of his thinking, you would hear something like this: *There she goes again. Must be that time of the month…hormonal imbalance. Oh well, she'll get over it. She'll see that I'm right. She has such limited insight. It's hard for her to handle the truth.* Yikes!

So close, but… What Louis didn't get was that Francine feels lonely and misunderstood in this relationship, and that his angry tone and demeaning treatment are unacceptable and she won't tolerate them anymore. He probably isn't even aware that Francine understands his inability to express his needs and desires openly without feeling weak or ashamed. He didn't hear that she would love to share more time and intimacy with him, but that it's impossible for her to wrap her arms around the fire-breathing dragon he's become. He didn't get to hear that she feels hurt, even though she knows he probably doesn't mean to hurt her, and that she needs him to be more responsible for the impact of his words and tone. He doesn't understand that although she knows he loves her, that simply isn't good enough anymore. And he never heard her admit that she has colluded in this dysfunctional pattern of relating because of the issues in her own life, but that she isn't going to play along anymore. He wasn't held accountable for his actions.

Louis demands excessive special attention from Francine. He can't appreciate the unreasonable nature of his unrelenting expectations. Nina Brown, an expert on narcissism, writes, "Everyone can appreciate feeling unique and special from time to time. Indeed, one of the reasons we fall in love or become attracted to someone is their ability to make us feel that way. However, the person who has an excessive need to feel unique and special expects *everyone* to make them feel that way all of the time. They can be easily displeased or even angered when others do not act to make them feel unique and special" (2001, 27).

Unfortunately, Francine wasn't directly engaged in a confrontation with Louis and his unreasonable demands and unremitting criticisms. She was engaged in a phantom war. She was the frightened little girl whose mother left and whose father worked all the time, who had to sacrifice her needs and desires so that she could take good care of her little sister. That little girl, now turned feisty and defiant, was doing battle with the long-held belief that she must suck it up. No matter how justified her feelings, the way she expressed herself ultimately didn't serve what she needs and wants to communicate in the present, and she wasn't responding to Louis in the here and now. Instead, she was just falling into an old pattern. As she works to summon new strength, she needs to correct the errors in thoughts and behaviors that no longer serve her so she can fight the battle to be waged in the here and now, with Louis, who often exasperates her and who would test anyone's interpersonal skills. Remember, almost no one can push people's buttons like the narcissist can.

This is not to say that the failed communication was Francine's fault. She was doing the best she could, given that this has always been one of her most challenging and important relationships. She's working hard to believe that she matters and that she doesn't have anything to prove anymore. She's struggling to obtain emotional reciprocity from Louis. The ratio of give to get in their relationship has been off for as long as she's known him, and she's begun to recognize her responsibility for this, having discreetly agreed to surrender and sacrifice her own needs in the hope that he would change, that one day he would come to appreciate her and love her better.

Francine has felt trapped for years, being a teacher with a minimal income and the mother of two children. She was committed to raising her sons in an intact family, sparing them the sorrows of growing up in a broken home, as she had. Her liabilities and fears were her anchors; she wouldn't run as her mother had. For a long time, she had felt herself to be a virtuous victim for putting up with Louis. Now she's struggling to be compassionate with herself, given her limited options, her fear, and her genuine (but dimming) love for this man who has been so disappointing to her in so many ways.

Francine, like many spouses of narcissists, believes in the underlying goodness of her partner. She's witnessed his stumbling efforts to tell her he loves her and to look after her when she's had to face difficult losses, medical issues, and depression. She knows his story and feels a deep love for the vulnerable part of him who lives in exile. But it isn't her responsibility, nor is it within her power, to change Louis. She may light the torch and lead the way for a while, in which case her openness and example may have a significant impact on the path he ultimately chooses. But she doesn't intend to carry the burden indefinitely without seeing improvements in Louis's emotional intimacy, reciprocity, respect, and empathy.

A Game of Collusion

Psychotherapist Sandy Hotchkiss, an expert in personality disorders, writes, "For narcissists, competition of all kinds is a way to reaffirm superiority, although many will only compete when they anticipate a favorable outcome" (2003, 13). Louis, knowing Francine's tendency to get choked up in the midst of a plea for tenderness and fair play, could easily mow her down with a lofty rendition of theories on gender differences and displaced female angst. He's long been a solid victor at the game of never getting her point and never feeling her pain. He's always been able to count on her business-as-usual behavior once things cooled down. In fact, he's been a master at this game with most of the people in his life. His assistant, Beth, who worked for him for ten years, tells the story of how Louis could make you doubt the very color of the blouse you were wearing, even if it was undoubtedly green to anyone's eye. His personal trainer, Bill, tells of times when Louis would keep him waiting for nearly twenty minutes, then inevitably convince him that it was the rigid policy of the gym that was faulty, not Louis's time management.

What do all three of these people—Francine, Beth, and Bill—have in common that allows Louis to be such an unstoppable and disarming champ in their interactions? In his presence, all three of them frequently experience intimidation, resignation, and disillusioned self-doubt. Though Louis's personality is a big factor, Francine, Beth, and Bill all have their own schemas that play a role in creating the painful dynamic of their relationships with Louis. Let's take a closer look at Beth and Bill to illuminate this common thread. As you read through their stories, try to identify any elements that feel relevant to your experience with the narcissist in your life.

Bill, the Trainer

Bill frequently falls victim not to Louis, but to his own personal traps of failure, subjugation, and defectiveness. He is triggered by Louis's colossal vocabulary, his deep and sonorous voice, and the impressive financial accomplishments Louis boasts of during his stretches and cooldown sessions. Because he fears rejection by Louis or being made to feel he isn't as smart or as well versed in the gym's policies, Bill pushes his own opinions to the far corners of his mind.

His experiences with Louis trigger the all-too-familiar memory of being teased and bullied for not being able to keep up with the more aggressive kids in the schoolyard. Pressured to put up or shut up when it came to competition, he chose to shut up—probably a good decision back then, given that Bill had no real advocate to guide or protect him. Bill's dad was a workaholic who was never around, and his mom was very ill during much of his childhood. His grandma told him that he was a good boy but a bit too weak, just like his grandpa, who died when Bill was a baby. All of these discordant melodies from his childhood continue to resonate in his thirty-two-year-old brain, and the automatic reflex to dodge enemies from his distant past emerges once again. Bill forgets that he's an amazing personal trainer, well respected by his peers and clients alike. While he would like to maintain Louis as his client, he doesn't need to tolerate his disrespect and self-righteous domination. The smell, sound, and feel of something old and familiar capture Bill, anchoring him to the early chapters of his childhood story.

Beth, the Administrative Assistant

Beth, a forty-four-year-old woman who has risen in the ranks of the company that brought so much fame and fortune to Louis, is a bright and hardworking person who generously gives of her time and creative energy both at work and at home. Despite her own prestigious education and high achievements, Beth's ego is all too easily erased in the face of powerful authority figures. Louis was one such figure. Her father was another.

Beth grew up in a small town within a fairly large family. She was the youngest of five children and the pièce de résistance in her father's eyes. In fact, finding hiding places from her father's ever-present gaze was quite the challenge for young Beth. Her dad demanded a great deal of attention from her and denied her the ordinary and reasonable privileges of a young girl. He was unrelenting in his expectations that she should be the best at everything. As an adolescent, Beth was a bit of a jouster, and when she disagreed with her father, making her opposing point of view and pleas for a normal life loud and clear, her temerity in challenging her father's "wisdom" and authority was met by his smoldering stare, heartbroken displeasure, and irrefutably punitive voice. Because she enjoyed her father's fondness and feared the guilt she felt when she upset him, Beth eventually resigned herself to gazing up at the pedestal she placed him on, trading her personal needs for maintaining peace in his heart, much like her mom had done.

Beth earned many honors and much recognition throughout her early academic life, including being valedictorian of her high school class and receiving merit scholarships for college. She often recalled the proud look on her father's face—an immigrant whose dream was to see his children go to college and have a better life than his own—when she strode by him in her cap and gown on graduation day. In a brief interview, she told me, "In that moment it felt like it was worth all the loneliness, not choosing my own clothes, and all the missed parties, dates, and movies to see the happiness I could bring that man by being what he needed me to be."

So what's wrong with that story, you might ask? Perhaps it's the lack of balance—and the lack of an authentically defined self. Beth stated that her emotional legacy was an inability to have a genuine sense of herself and a tendency to always feel she had to be what others needed her to be, which left her constantly running from guilt for letting people down or disappointing them. She even feared that she might bequeath these traits to her daughters. Even now, when she runs into Louis at a social event, Beth can feel tightness in her stomach and nervousness in her throat as she prepares her curtsy for the mighty master, ready to agree with whatever he might utter.

Wendy, the Therapist

Okay, now it's my turn. Early in therapy, Louis had a predictable habit of being five to ten minutes late and then demanding more time at the end of the session. "What's the big deal about giving me five to ten more minutes? This is important! You see, you're just like every other therapist, or even lawyers for that matter. It's a business: time's up, pay up. I feel I should have a few extra minutes when I need it." Sometimes he would just ignore me and continue to talk right past my announcement that the session was over. Given that many therapists tend to have self-sacrifice or subjugation schemas, or both, the task of being assertive and setting limits can be an onerous one.

I had to find a way to push past my anger at Louis's sense of entitlement, as well as my guilt for not giving in to his demands for extra time. Finally, I harnessed my awareness of little Louis and his need to feel special in order to feel cared for, along with his experience of getting his way for many years, and told him, "Louis, if what you mean is that I couldn't possibly care about you given the time limitations of our session, consider this: You can only pay me for my time and expertise; the caring is free. Even *you* cannot *make* me care about you. And I must tell you that when you speak to me as you just did, it's hard for me to feel my caring for you. I wonder if this is what it's like for Francine and your sons."

Trying to communicate to Louis that I didn't view the situation as his fault, but that I did see his behavior as his responsibility, I said, "I know it's hard for you, given that no one has ever helped you tolerate feelings of disappointment or frustration, and because you were led to believe that you were superior to other people and entitled to special privileges. You were taught that the rules for everyone else don't really apply to you. So it isn't your fault, Louis. But in order to have the kinds of relationships you long for, you must work on these beliefs and behaviors or you'll keep driving people away from you. Let's try it again: tell me about the disappointment you feel when our time is up."

Louis, who managed to listen with a minimum of eye-rolling, sighed and, with difficulty, replied, "The time seems to go by very quickly, and sometimes—okay, often—I want to be here longer, to finish a thought or to tell you about something else, and it's frustrating to have to stop when you say so. I end up feeling like I'm being rejected or controlled, even though I do believe that you're trying to help me." I thanked him for his courageous openness and assured him that I understood why he felt that way, given his life themes and the inherent limitations of a therapy relationship.

I asked him, "How uncomfortable was it for you to say it that way, Louis?" He replied, "It's just unnatural, and I have to think about it. It's tedious and a little annoying." Even Louis smirked at having said this, recognizing the arrogance of the statement. I suggested that it's an unfamiliar way of being in the world, one that requires paying closer attention to the feelings of listeners, as well as his own unacknowledged and most important feelings—something he wasn't used to. Louis agreed with this assessment. I also let him know that it was hard for me to ask him to leave, but that it wouldn't be fair to my other clients if I didn't, as they would then have to wait. Then I reminded him that it was hard for me to care for him when I felt like he was ignoring my rights and criticizing my intentions unfairly. Louis nodded. He got it. We then collaborated on a plan for setting our agenda a bit differently, mindful of time limitations and his vulnerability. In addition, Louis agreed to make a better effort to arrive on time for his sessions.

In schema therapy, leverage is important for working successfully with narcissists. Jeffrey Young describes it like this: "The therapist strives to keep patients in touch with their emotional suffering because as soon as the suffering is gone, they are likely to leave treatment. The more the therapist keeps patients aware of their inner emptiness, feelings of defectiveness, and loneliness, the more the therapist has leverage for keeping them in treatment... The therapist also focuses on the negative consequences of the patient's narcissism, such as rejection by loved ones or setbacks in one's career... The emotional connection to the therapist and fear of reprisal from others are the main motivators for continuing in therapy" (Young, Klosko, and Weishaar 2006, 395).

Exercise: The Burden, Not the Blame

Are you ready to take on the burden of change without the blame—to accept that even if your schemas aren't your fault, you are responsible for your behavior now, as an adult? Though it may seem a bit scary or overwhelming, this also opens the door to the potential for transformation. This exercise will help you examine your own schemas and coping modes and identify healthy and assertive ways of responding to replace old patterns of behavior. This will be inherently good for you, and there's a good chance that your clear communication will help improve your relationship with the narcissist. In this exercise, you'll also consider any leverage you might have for getting the attention of the narcissist in your life and pq person for change. Here's an example:

Your schemas: *Abandonment, defectiveness, self-sacri... subjugation.*

Effects of your schemas: *I take the blame, feel inadequate, and believe that it's better to put my needs on the back burner and be silent than to speak out, get it wrong, and possibly end up all alone.*

Your coping modes: *Giving in and avoiding.*

The truth: *It isn't my fault. We both play a role in the conflict. I am capable of being responsible, and besides, I'm already so alone because I don't have a sense of self, a voice, or a meaningful connection with my husband.*

Healthy assertive message: *I will not be treated this way. It's unacceptable, even if it isn't your intention to hurt me.*

Leverage: *I know that my husband doesn't want to lose me. I'm willing to start communicating about the option of leaving—not as a threat, but as a necessary choice if things don't change between us.*

Using the structure set forth in that example, take a fresh piece of paper and write about your own schemas and coping modes, then consider the truth of the situation. Take some time to develop a healthy assertive message—one that neither cowers before the narcissist in your life nor attacks that person viciously. Finally, take some time to consider what leverage you might bring to bear to enlist the narcissist in making changes to improve your relationship.

Hope Springs Eternal: The Capacity to Learn and Change

Without the unlikely intervention of magic, the options for resolving conflicts in relationships are finite: ending the relationship, sticking with the status quo, adopting new dysfunctional patterns, or working it out in a healthy way. The last of these is obviously best if you wish to stay in the relationship, but it requires an exhausting commitment, even when both parties are fully enlisted in the process of change. But rest assured: all is not lost. While the challenge may seem daunting, the possibilities for repair are real.

The brain is capable of change, and therefore our personalities are flexible and open to change as well. Experts in mental health, along with those who study the brain, propose that one pathway to change may come from attuned listening and genuine self-expression within the context of a conscious, here-and-now state of mind. Dan Siegel uses the term "contingent communication" to describe this approach: "In contingent communication the receiver of the message listens with an open mind and with all his or her senses. Her reaction is dependent on what was actually communicated, not on a predetermined and rigid mental model of what was expected" (Siegel and Hartzell 2004, 81).

Siegel goes on to illustrate the essence of "feeling felt" in terms of the parent-child relationship: "When we send out a signal, our brains are receptive to the responses of others to that signal. The responses we receive become embedded in the neural maps of our core sense of self… The responses of others are not merely mirrors of our own signals but incorporate the essence of the other person's view, which makes sense of our communication. In this manner, children come to feel felt: they come to feel as if their mind exists in the mind of their parent" (Siegel and Hartzell 2004, 83). What a soothing connection—to feel truly "gotten," to sense that you are held accurately and safely in the mind of another. Think about it: Who truly gets you?

Conclusion

Within the context of "felt" connections, we are afforded the chance to achieve mental and emotional shifts that lead to new interpretations and actions regarding self-worth and our relationships with others. These connections offer us the possibility of forming new habits and freeing ourselves from automatic reflexes linked to the past. So the task is to establish this sort of connection with the narcissist in your life, whether that person is a boss, coworker, family member, neighbor, friend, spouse, or lover.

Unfortunately, these last two are usually the most resistant to change, given the enormity of importance of the relationship and how heartily entrenched your schemas may be for both of you. But by establishing a more "felt" connection, you open the door to repairing your sense of self, and to the possibility of utilizing your repertoire of skills to improve and transform your relationship with the narcissist or, if that isn't possible, limiting the relationship or even ending it. To this end, the following chapters will help you sharpen your awareness, harness your courage, and maintain your enthusiasm while developing the skills you need for creating effective outcomes when dealing with the narcissist in your life.

chapter 4

Overcoming the Obstacles: Communication Pitfalls, Snags, and Glitches

It is one of the most beautiful compensations of life that no man can sincerely try to help another without helping himself.

—Ralph Waldo Emerson

You now have a framework for understanding narcissism: how to define it, how it affects the lives of narcissists, and how that acerbic behavior impacts those who must deal with these people (something you were probably all too familiar with already). The earlier chapters have given you a glimpse of the origins of narcissism and a conceptual understanding of these challenging people. Previous chapters have also provided a background in several fields of psychological science that inform a strategy for changing your relationship with the narcissist. This strategy typically involves four stages:

1. **Observation:** You observe the specific behaviors, reactions, and interactions that characterize the relationship between you and the narcissist.

2. **Assessment:** Your observations and insights allow you to assess the dynamics in your relationship more accurately and perhaps more dispassionately.

3. **Identification:** Your assessment enables you to name the schemas that provoke ineffective responses—for both you and the narcissist—and to recognize the coping responses both of you are using.

4. **Differentiation:** Your identification of the schemas and coping responses at play allow you to differentiate experiences driven by memory and temperament from here-and-now moments, liberating an authentic, sturdy, and credible voice for each of you.

Four Stages of Transformation

You may find journaling a useful adjunct to this process—and helpful in general. Writing in a journal can be a very soothing activity. It can also help you find a new perspective on dysfunctional interactions and provide a place where you might begin to express your authentic voice, rehearsing for real-world interactions. In regard to the four-stage process discussed here, it can help with differentiation, allowing you to see the biased thoughts and emotions flooding your brain as they emerge on the page before you. An example of the four stages might look something like this:

1. **Observation:** You notice that your relationship with the narcissist is one where you do most of the giving and he does most of the getting—especially getting his own way. Whereas you're prone to feeling guilty and apologizing for

your limitations, he's more likely to make excuses and blame others for his bad behavior.

2. **Assessment:** You can see how the lack of balance in the relationship and your sense of its unfairness are linked to feelings of anxiety and despair. These feelings have a familiar resonance that's connected to some of the earliest chapters in your life story.

3. **Identification:** With your new understanding of early maladaptive schemas, you can see how your emotional deprivation, defectiveness, self-sacrifice, and subjugation schemas are the culprits behind these weighted feelings. You can see that you didn't receive an adequate amount of support and emotional nurturing as a child and that you always had a sense of never being good enough, causing you to build a sturdy fortress out of doing and giving. This helped you numb the throbbing ache of longing for love and approval—a longing you perceived as shameful. If you happen to know the childhood history of the narcissist in your life, or perhaps by using what you've gleaned from this book, you can also connect the dots to name his schemas and begin to see patterns in the choreography of his undesirable moves.

4. **Differentiation:** The art of knowing the difference between what was and what is, differentiation allows you to be in your mind and your body in real time—in the here and now. Armed with the knowledge of which schemas and coping patterns are involved in the dynamics of your relationship, you can lay down your word weaponry. You recognize that you are no longer a powerless child, but rather a capable adult who can take a stand without hiding, blaming, or caving in.

Here's a simple example of how your authentic, sturdy, and credible voice might sound when negotiating with your partner about your desire to change a well-established routine: "I know you enjoy watching your favorite TV shows on Thursday night. It also happens to be the one weeknight we don't have to work late and could possibly do something fun together, such as have a date night. Could we perhaps do that once or twice a month? You could record your programs on those nights. We often end up arguing about Thursday night activities and I always end up giving in. I'd really appreciate it if we could agree on a compromise that allows for other options. I believe we fight over this because you've grown accustomed to my consistent support and my acceptance of your criticisms regarding my suggestions for fun. I guess I haven't been aware of how I resented that, and how much I need your support as well."

Here's another example, this time using an interaction with a supervisor: "It's not very easy for me to say this because I'm aware of my long-standing tendency to do what I'm told, even if I don't agree or if I have another, possibly better solution. Sometimes I'm overly invested in your approval of me. However, I want to propose that we improve our marketing efforts in this way... I also think that you and I should have regularly scheduled meetings to measure the progress on this project. The current process leaves me feeling invisible and sometimes unfairly criticized, even though I'm sure that isn't your intention."

Given your past experiences with the narcissist in your life, you may wonder whether such an approach will actually work. Here's another example that proves it can. A client named Carolyn had married a narcissistic man, Damian, and inherited his narcissistic seventeen-year-old daughter, Lucy—Daddy's prideful princess, with his prized pedigree and an often prickly mood. During her visits, Lucy could woo her father into giving her whatever she wanted and letting her off the hook. There were no rules or consequences, even when Lucy spoke disrespectfully to Carolyn, borrowed things from Carolyn's closet without asking, or sabotaged Carolyn and Damian's plans for a night out. Lucy never showed any appreciation, never cooperated, and felt no qualms about racking up countless credit card charges.

Carolyn felt helpless—not surprising, given Damian's harsh decree: "My daughter, my rules, period." But eventually, despite Carolyn's devastating fear of another failed marriage, she worked up enough courage to advocate for her rights in her home and told Damian that if things didn't change, she was leaving. Although Carolyn didn't expect it at the time, this new, assertive approach created the leverage needed for change. After several bouts of typical behavior, in which Damian proclaimed, "Who cares! Go right ahead and leave," he actually agreed to enter therapy and work on these issues with Carolyn and with Lucy. Carolyn will ultimately choose or not choose to stay in this marriage now that she's no longer at the mercy of her abandonment and shame monsters.

Cues and Clues: Knowing Why You Get Triggered

The past informs the present, awakening mind's automatic mechanisms for identifying threatening conditions and steering us to safety. Think back to chapter 3, where you learned about the coping responses Francine, Beth, and Bill exhibited when their early maladaptive schemas were triggered by Louis's challenging behaviors. With time and guidance, each of them learned to identify the resonantly uncomfortable physical and mental sensations that arose when confronted with his incorrigibility. Each learned to link this familiar distress to relevant schemas archived in their stories from the past. They soon noticed that the familiarity of sensations triggering their schemas seemed to automatically drive their correspondingly familiar, though ineffective, responses.

Exercise: Why the Narcissist Triggers *You*

If you haven't already identified your own schemas, go back to chapter 2 and take a moment to review the list again. See if you can find those schemas that most accurately represent the themes of your life. Keep in mind that in order for it to be an early maladaptive schema, it must have roots in your childhood or adolescence. And, though it may have been dormant throughout much of your life, it's pertinent enough that you feel it acutely as you read about it now. Go ahead and list your schemas on a piece of paper.

With an awareness of your schemas firmly in mind, proceed with the following exercise. Because it involves a guided visualization, you'll need to read through it first to familiarize yourself with the steps before actually doing them.

1. Find a quiet place where you won't be interrupted and sit comfortably. Close your eyes for a moment. Try to recall a painful childhood memory involving one of your caregivers, a sibling, or someone from your peer group. Assign a part of you to act as a sentry—remaining keenly watchful of your feet firmly planted on the ground, safely anchored to this moment, here and now—so that you can permit yourself to gently look back and notice the thoughts, feelings, and sensations that emerge as you call up this difficult event. What happened during this painful event? How did you deal with it? Can you recall what you wish had happened at that time? What were your deepest longings? If recalling the experience becomes difficult or painful, remind yourself that you are only remembering.

2. Take a slow, deep breath in and then slowly exhale completely. Blank out the images of that past event but continue to hold on to the thoughts, emotions, and sensations that fill your mind and body. Keep them with you, allowing your soft and gentle breath to caress any painful associations etched on the walls of your mind.

3. Now that you've honed an awareness of difficult thoughts, emotions, and sensations and experienced how your breath can help ease their impact, call up a picture of the narcissist in your life. See if you can zoom in on a difficult, upsetting,

or annoying encounter—past or potential. Make the i as vivid as possible within your mind. Pay attention thoughts, emotions, and physical sensations that resonate as this charged scenario unfolds within you. If you could control the outcome, what do you wish would happen? What are your deepest longings?

4. Take a couple of slow, gentle breaths, in and out, then open your eyes and give yourself a moment to become fully reengaged with your surroundings. Say thank you to the part of you that kept you safely grounded so that you could make the journey.

After you complete the practice, compare the thoughts, emotions, and physical sensations associated with the first image—your memory from childhood—with those of the second. Was there a shift, or were they consistent? The difference between your experience of the two visualizations indicates the degree to which your capacity to observe, assess, identify, and differentiate has emerged. Turning your awareness to your internal experience during these scenarios also allows you to measure the strength of your schemas and how entrenched old, maladaptive coping modes are when activated by current conditions.

When you compare your internal experience in these two scenarios, do you see any patterns? How have your longings changed since that childhood experience, if at all? What do you continue to long for? What keeps you from getting those desires met? There's a lot to consider here. You may wish to take some time to write about your thoughts and feelings to help you sort through your emotions. Doing so may also be useful in the future, allowing you to gauge your progress.

Finally, take a look at the list of your schemas one more time. Do you feel reasonably confident that you've accurately identified those most pertinent to your life story—those that may be implicitly interfering with your own interpersonal effectiveness? If so, good for you. If not, don't worry. This is a complex task, and you may have multiple layers of history and behavioral patterns to unfold. Read on; there is much more ahead that will assist you in your discovery.

Making Sense of Our Senses: Messages from the Brain and Body

As you now know, sometimes your schemas will be triggered (often outside of your awareness), sounding the chime for less-than-impressive responses as your soldiers of self-preservation report for duty. There are also plenty of times when you successfully bypass activation of your schemas and maturely respond to the challenges of your life with wise restraint or a clever riposte, as needed. If this is seldom possible when dealing with the narcissist in your life, rest assured that you're not alone; these challenging folks seem to have a knack for triggering people's schemas. The reasons this is the case for you are perhaps clearer now that you've begun to uncover your private collection of life themes and corresponding coping styles. Though these coping styles may not have served you well, arming you for confrontation or fastening you to the frozen tundra of resignation, they can provide valuable clues about your cognitive and sensory system, and as such are essential guideposts along the way to healthy emancipation.

Take a moment to recall the potent sensations you experienced in the previous exercise while recalling a painful page from your personal narrative. As you landed upon that dismal memory, the sensations in your mind and body swelled and took on a power entirely out of proportion with the reality of the actual situation in the here and now, where you were sitting alone, quietly, with eyes closed. Such is the sway of schemas; they are woven into your sensory system and can initiate forceful and intense sensations when they are triggered.

The sensory system includes your muscles, nervous system, and viscera. When your schemas are triggered, you may notice some combination of the following physical sensations:

- Increased heart rate

- Elevated blood pressure

- Increased skin temperature

- Faster breathing rate

- A damp brow or palms

- A queasy or achy feeling in your stomach

- Tightness or a lump in your throat

- Dry mouth

- Quivering lips

- Tingling in your hands, feet, or legs

- A sudden stiffness in your neck, back, or joints

- Dizziness

- Welling of tears

- Sleepiness

- Pain or numbness in parts of your body

- Your mind going blank

- A heightening or dulling of your senses: sound, smell, visual recognition, taste, or touch

Why is this relevant? Because schemas, in cahoots with your sensory system, send messages from the body to the brain and vice versa, setting off internal but often false alarms to arouse you to self-protective action. The problem here is that the brain can be fooled. It can't easily differentiate between a stomachache brought on by a virus and one brought on by a marathon melee with the narcissist. And further, it is prone to associating either of these

rgettable stomachaches in first grade at parochial
1 were terrorized by the threat of burning in the
forgot to wear your beanie, thus tilling the soil for
1r mistrust schema.

lful attunement to your inner state and structure,
subtle and not-so-subtle sensory stimuli can leave you feeling suspicious and on edge anytime you feel queasy. If, on the other hand, you can make sense out of the uneasy feeling in your stomach, attributing it to a definite physical cause (*I have a nauseous feeling in my stomach because I caught the bug that everyone in my office has had all week, not because danger lurks ahead*), you might be able to put self-doubts aside and simply rest if you are unwell. Alternatively, you might start to see a pattern of nonphysical causes (*I have a nauseous feeling in my stomach every time I get into it with my coworker Sherry because I wind up feeling like Sister Joseph Marie is about to toss me down the chute to hell without my sunscreen*), in which case you might be able to garner your courage and stand up to Sherry with sturdiness and conviction. To be successful in this, you must invite your brain to download a new mantra: *That was then and this is now.* Chapter 5 will give you many tools for making the distinction and living by that mantra.

Exercise: Anticipating the Glitches and Activating Your Radar

Now that you've learned about the insidious ways in which schemas can activate painful emotions and distressing physical sensations, you're probably eager to learn how to short-circuit this response. Building on the previous exercise, this one also uses a visualization of a difficult encounter with your narcissist. Here, you'll begin to practice new awareness skills in the relative comfort and safety of your own mind, rather than one-on-one with the narcissist. You'll also gain some experience in using a positive and compassionate inner dialogue to place your schemas in perspective.

1. Think about your next encounter with the narcissist. When and where will it occur? What will the circumstances of this meeting be?

2. Think about all of the possible interpersonal challenges that might arise during this encounter.

3. Take into account all that you can possibly predict about how you're likely to feel, given the importance of the particular activity that brings you together, your typical level of sensitivity in such situations, and historical precedents in this type of situation. Consider everything from peripheral distractions to the worst-case scenario.

4. Bring your attention to the sensations in your body and the thoughts moving through your mind. Point the radar of your awareness to your most vulnerable areas of sensitivity—those deep red thunderstorms embedded in the rainy background.

5. If your senses could talk, what would they be saying? For example, if you have a defectiveness schema combined with a punitive coping mode, the tightness in your neck might say, *You're such a wimp; you can't even defend yourself.* Look at the sensations you're experiencing and try to identify what they're saying to you.

6. Allow your wise and compassionate inner voice to engage those sensations in a dialogue. For example, you might say, *I was often made to feel that I wasn't good enough when I was young, but that just wasn't true. I was only a child. I had no capacity to stand up for myself then. I was young and scared. What I'm experiencing now is the resonance of that schema. But I have choices right now. I don't have to tolerate being treated this way by anyone anymore.*

7. Notice how the sensations triggered by your imaginary encounter with the narcissist begin to slowly make their exit. If you can't come up with words to refute your schema, you might ask a friend, loved one, therapist, or anyone who really knows you

to help you compose an authentic message that reflects your inner truth.

Having activated your internal radar, you can now scan your internal world for distorting schemas, those nemeses of truth. Later in the chapter, you'll learn more communication skills and get more chances to rehearse for successful interactions with the narcissist in your life.

Charmed and Disarmed

As you may recall, the narcissist has the unremitting power to intoxicate your senses with his aura of charm and beguiling wit. He can make you feel like you're the chosen one, that you must be very special to have garnered his attention. And just as you begin to swell under his spell, you find yourself squinting in the dark for the exit sign. He will get you the best seat in the house for his swaggering performance. In return, you're expected to hold the spotlight steadily upon him, nod affirmatively during his orations, laugh on cue, never appear to be bored, applaud loudly and frequently, and never, ever expect to join him on the stage.

Bait and Switch Maneuvers

The narcissist's charm is an enticing lure. It's also an effective tool, as it may keep you from examining the potential costs of the relationship until you're hooked. Let's take a look at some specific examples of the subtle but classic bait and switch maneuvers narcissists use. This might help you gain a clearer perspective on the dynamic in your own relationship with a narcissist.

The vanishing act. After promising you his undying attention, the narcissist becomes unavailable. With no acknowledgment or contrition, he accuses you of being selfish and needy when you feel upset about it.

The setup. Having solicited your ideas and input with seeming enthusiasm, the narcissist proceeds to assassinate your response and annihilate your self-esteem with demeaning criticisms.

Dr. Jekyll and Mr. Hyde. Seizing the opportunity to be your hero, the narcissist will be abundantly protective when others are unfair to you. But he will have no compunction about cutting you to the quick with his harsh and lordly tones if you dare to interrupt him or question his opinions.

Adding insult to injury. The narcissist will show up unexpectedly with a truckload of roses, making you feel disposed to forgive his cloddish behavior of the past few days. You reciprocate with acts of love and appreciation, but, ultimately, nothing is ever enough for his chasm of insatiability, leaving you grinding your teeth between guilt and exasperation. Eventually, it's all about him again.

Devil's advocate. Like the president of a debate club or a judge with gavel in hand, the narcissist invites you into a conversation that quickly becomes either a long drawn-out soliloquy, argumentative, or highly competitive. No matter what your response—ignoring him, fighting back, pleading, or even giving in—he is impervious.

Do any of these maneuvers sound familiar? If all of them do, don't despair. Many of my clients who are dealing with this issue report that all five are often relevant. Remember, the narcissist maintains very high, unrelenting standards for himself, and for those who orbit his stellar magnificence. As you have also learned, narcissists have an extremely high need for recognition, approval, control, victory, and acknowledgment of their extraordinariness. They have these needs because of a fierce inner current of shame, emotional loneliness, and mistrust. Self-righteous behavior is merely a plug in the emotional dam.

Typical Emotional Responses

Clearly, the narcissist doesn't feel bound to play by the same rules as the rest of us. These bait and switch maneuvers are unfair and duplicitous, and worse, the narcissist's personality doesn't allow an opening for calling the behavior into question or negotiating a solution, compounding the situation. In the absence of fair communication and negotiation, each of the maneuvers tends to elicit a specific response.

Insecurity. When the narcissist is performing his vanishing act, the instability of his mood and unreliability of his presence may leave you feeling alone and insecure. This feeling sometimes harkens back to memories of unstable relationships during your childhood.

Intimidation. The setup maneuver can be downright intimidating, like being gently coaxed to dip your toe into the water only to have it bitten by a piranha. This maneuver can often mimic childhood scenarios, such as your parent encouraging you to choose something from a dinner menu and then criticizing you for the choice you made. In response, you learned how to read between the lines to find the "right" answer, even if it wasn't necessarily your own.

Resentment. When the narcissist transforms from Dr. Jekyll into the odious Mr. Hyde, you become resentful of his superiority, selfishness, and inability to compromise, especially if only fifteen minutes ago he was heroically defending you. Suddenly his support and heroic efforts don't feel like they're about you at all. This can feel like those rare times when your mother would call you from your room and invite you to join her at the table where she was entertaining friends. It was nice to feel included and wanted, but within moments you realized that this was just a ploy so she could bask in everyone's oohs and aahs over what a beautiful job she'd done with you. Once again, you were left dutifully holding the spotlight on her "mother of the year" act.

Provocation. How does the narcissist manage to be so charming when heaping insult atop injury? And why do you fall for it every time? It isn't because you're foolish, but because it feels good to be cared for and have moments when you're treated kindly. You go out on a limb to be appreciative of the narcissist's gallantry, only to find that the charming prince you've kissed is really a frog. You feel provoked that you were once again captured by his miniature moments of magic and forced to pay the price with yet another predictable case of warts. This may be reminiscent of a dynamic with your parents; perhaps you savored the all-too-rare loving attention your mother showered on you when you were ill, only to be guilt-tripped because she lost sleep while taking care of you.

Powerlessness. The devil's advocate maneuver is primarily a way of elevating the uniqueness of whatever the narcissist is orating about, leaving you feeling powerless and weary. You feel like it's a no-win situation; if you don't concede, he'll keep you up all night, making his point endlessly and enjoying the sound of his own voice. This can sometimes feel like the powerlessness of being a child, especially if you learned to subjugate your voice to a parent or caregiver who wanted you to keep your ideas and opinions to yourself and respect her point of view as sacrosanct.

In all of these scenarios, you are inherently primed to protect yourself but end up feeling provoked, insecure, intimidated, resentful, or powerless—ironically, quite unprotected. Why? To understand this, we need to revisit how the brain works. When confronted by a grizzly bear, your mechanisms for survival are limited. You may try to run from the bear, you may try to fight him off, or you may just stand there, frozen in fear, unable to move in any direction—typical fight, flight, or freeze responses. In schema therapy, we refer to these survival mechanisms as counterattack, avoidance, and surrender. For some people, the response often depends on the nature of the threat. For others, the response to any threat may always seem to be the same.

The Low Road

In conversations with Dan Siegel, he has helped me understand that when the brain senses a threat, the lower subcortical portions (the brain stem and limbic areas) become activated. Once the assessment of a threat is received by these subcortical areas, including a part known as the amygdala, messages are transmitted to the body to create a sense of distress and ready you for action. Part of the response involves a discharge of excitatory hormones, such as adrenaline. This all occurs very rapidly. This hardwired system engages in a fight, flight, or freeze response that is invaluable for survival for most animals (including humans) when confronting a truly dangerous or life-threatening situation.

Dan Siegel has proposed what he calls a "low road" of function in which a state of threat can sometimes shut off the higher functions of the prefrontal cortex. This prefrontal area serves as the chief executive officer of your brain, helping to soothe your mind, regulate your body, engage in thoughtful reasoning, and reflect clearly and insightfully on what's going on. Immersion in the low road means a loss of these executive functions. Without prefrontal reflection, you might not be able to recognize that a bump in the night is simply hot water moving through the pipes and not an intruder sneaking up the stairs. Siegel's work offers a way to both understand and gain control over these low road experiences in our lives (Siegel 2001, 2007; Siegel and Hartzell 2004).

Interacting with the narcissist can sometimes activate both a perception of threat and immersion in the low road. But with reflection, you can interact with a narcissist without engaging in his dance. So instead of experiencing palpitations, headaches, and a dry mouth whenever in close proximity to the don or the diva, driven by anticipation of yet another confrontation that will hit you like an oncoming bus, you might actually show up with confidence, a sense of self-worth, and authenticity.

Beyond Fight, Flight, or Freeze

Achieving effective results in your interactions with a narcissist requires modifications to the choreography of your survival system. To help you adjust your internal alarms, let's take a look at some typical fight, flight, and freeze responses, how these responses can be modified, and how to most effectively communicate from this new stance.

Counterattack (the fight response): If you're prone to fighting back when you feel ignored or verbally attacked, your inner dialogue is one of *I'll show you*. This, of course, usually results in a wearying battle, a heightened verbal onslaught, or increased withdrawal on the part of your opponent.

Modification: Fighters need not give up the fight. You just need to stand up for yourself without attacking. For example, instead of *I'll show you*, your inner dialogue can become *I have rights too*.

Communication: Your new approach might sound like this: "Though it probably isn't your intention, I feel devalued by your actions and words. I won't tolerate being treated so disrespectfully. If you're uncomfortable with me, you can tell me without putting me down or ignoring me. You have rights, and so do I. I'd appreciate it if you could speak to me with more consideration, and I'll do the same for you."

Avoidance (the flight response): If you're prone to running away when things are difficult, your inner dialogue is one of *See ya later*. But the more you avoid, the more your opponent pursues, demands, and persists. You end up feeling cornered, incapacitated, and abandoned by your own voice.

Modification: If you are someone who needs distance from disquieting exchanges, that's okay. But in order to resolve a conflict, you need to eventually return. Your inner dialogue might go from *See ya later* to *I need a time-out*.

Communication: Your new approach might sound like this: "I know that this issue is very important to you. It's also important to me, but I'm feeling flooded right now. I need some time alone to regroup and gather my thoughts so our conversation might be productive. Perhaps you could benefit from it too."

Surrender (the freeze response): If you're prone to becoming immobilized in interactions that feel threatening, your only means of releasing yourself from the narcissist's sticky grip is to give in, take the blame, and agree. Your inner dialogue is one of *You're right; it's all my fault.* Unfortunately, this often results in further criticism for your fragile and flawed disposition.

Modification: If you have a reflexive freeze response, you may find a rehearsed script helpful. Your inner dialogue may go from *It's all my fault* to *I may not be perfect, but it's not all my fault.*

Communication: Your new approach might sound like this: "It seems that you're upset with me, and when I sense that, I have a tendency to give up and give in. I know this makes you more upset, but that isn't my intention. I get triggered by these exchanges, but I'm working to strengthen my confidence. I'd appreciate it if you could be more thoughtful toward me. You have responsibilities in this relationship too."

Conclusion

You've seen how your life experiences and biological makeup account for the personally relevant schemas and reactions that become obstacles to effectively dealing with the narcissist. You've practiced activating your inner radar to anticipate when you might fall prey to old habits, and you've begun to learn how to attend to sensory information. Although we humans are equipped with reflexive responses for survival, we're also extraordinarily flexible. You've started to see how adapting your internal dialogues and adopting new approaches to communication can lead to a greater sense of self-advocacy and authenticity in difficult relationships, and also influence change in these relationships.

Chapter 5 will further hone your skills in attending to sensory information. You'll learn the value of mindful attention in building new habits and enhancing flexibility in communication. You'll also continue to compose new scripts for managing interpersonal transactions with a genuine voice.

chapter 5

Paying Attention: Facing Difficult Encounters with a Narcissist

Everything that we see is a shadow cast by that which we do not see.

— Martin Luther King Jr.

In your work with this book thus far, you've devoted time and effort to making sense out of your life, examining your various life themes, and understanding how your past experience contributes to your sometimes luminous and other times dusky personality. You've investigated the links between your experiences, inclinations, and schemas. You have a sense of why dealing with a narcissist is particularly difficult for you, as well as why you might be captivated by and drawn to these people. You can more precisely anticipate and recognize how and when you may get triggered, and you're equipped with a new set of skills for understanding yourself and the narcissist, and for beginning to communicate more effectively and authentically.

The next step is to fully ground yourself in the moment. You are undoubtedly familiar with the expression "in one ear and out the other." This expression is a great example of the power of the Teflon-coated brain. Sometimes things just seem to slide right out of awareness. This can actually be quite liberating, allowing us to let go of cacophonous orchestrations of the mind and memory in the moment. So when Ms. Knows-It-All-and-Does-No-Wrong gets in your face with one of her careless comments regarding a personally difficult issue in your life or goes off on another tangent about how wonderful she is (poorly disguised by sophomoric modesty), you access the Teflon-coated aspect of your brain. You press your internal "mute" button, power off your schemas, and take a full, unexasperated breath. You masterfully hold the narcissist accountable if appropriate, or you move on. Where your "noisy" mind formerly would have had you feeling flustered, furious, full of self-doubt, or helpless, your distress now slides away like a fluffy omelet departs a well-prepared pan.

Breaking Free from Your Mechanical Habits

A fully felt sense of who you are and how you came to be that way is a powerful tool in enabling successful outcomes. But to wield this tool most effectively, you'll need to develop some supporting skills. Chief among them is the ability to identify unhealthy habits and catch yourself in the act of engaging in them. This is key in opening the door to new ways of responding to and interacting with the narcissist in your life.

As part of the human condition, you're predisposed to seek that which is familiar and respond with learned, developed, and innate habitual behaviors. And while some of these habits are healthy and adaptive, others hold you hostage within the prison walls of emotionally and physically painful schemas. Therefore, it is essential to have a clear mental picture, along with a truly felt sensibility, of your inner life—particularly the vulnerable parts of yourself. A sense of compassion for yourself is also vital. This will allow you to shift your focus and responses when you feel your vulnerability. Instead of attempting to cope with the same old messages of *I'm unlovable, No one could ever meet my needs, I have no rights, It's my responsibility to make other people happy,* and the like, you can shift your focus to more realistic assessments, liberating your mind and body from the distress associated with these long-held and biased themes. Once you've deconstructed and revised these damaging thought patterns, you need to keep your new, more equitable reality at hand to ward off your schemas and the things that trigger them, particularly narcissistic people.

So how do you stay out of that old prison? You now know memory to be a powerful force within the brain. And as long as you have a memory, you'll have schemas to manage. But if your newly crafted wise and loving internal voice is an attentive and reasonable advocate, you'll have far fewer triggering moments, and if you are triggered your experiences will be less intense and you'll be able to recover more quickly. That is, perhaps, as good as it gets. And it isn't too bad, if you think about it—especially since you can't be attentive 24/7. At times you may slip into old habits and find yourself in your familiar prison cell, demanding to be heard, burying your head in your pillow, or numbly staring at the walls around you. But remember, it's only a slip, not an indication that you are inherently flawed or doomed to failure. With this perspective, you'll soon discover that you can hoist yourself up out of that old cell and back into the moment.

Let's look at an example. Say you're at a social event and encounter Mr. Life-of-the-Party-Can't-Even-Remember-Your Name. You slip into your formerly intimidated and anxious mode of *I have nothing to contribute, so I'll just keep my thoughts to myself.* You sense your upset vis-à-vis an ache in the pit of your stomach. This is your cue. Recognize the familiarity of this sensation and the beliefs attached to it. Take a few moments to direct a kind and soothing focus on your inner world, perhaps with a gentle, discreet stretch or a few easy breaths, and tune in to the words of the internal advocate that you have so masterfully crafted—the inner voice that can tell you the truth when you slip. Recall that you're just fine, and that your reaction is simply the old, nagging stuff of memory. Remember that you have rights and opinions, and that you're entitled to have a good time without having to pander to the ego of Mr. Obnoxious. Having taken care of your internal world, you can wisely maneuver yourself to limit your encounters with him, and when in his presence, you can maintain your voice and your integrity.

One of my clients came up with a clever metaphor in the midst of working on his issues of covert narcissism while also trying to change his eating habits. We were investigating his approval-seeking tendencies and the upset he felt whenever his very popular (and also narcissistic) colleague Joe was in close proximity: "Joe is the cheeseburger that I really *want*. If he would only accept me into his inner circle, then I would feel I was truly special. But I know that what I really *need*, and actually enjoy, is the chicken wrap—because I'm already special, and the way to take good care of me is to bring healthier people into my life. My mom didn't know how to take good care of me and make me feel loved and special for being me. I only want Joe to accept me because my schema has me feeling that I'm not good enough as I am, that I need to be extraordinary and hang out with the popular guys in order to truly matter. Joe is an elixir for the pain of my triggered feelings. But the truth is, Joe and I have nothing in common, so the best he could ever be is a prop in my life. I don't need props. I need friends."

The Power of Mindful Awareness

To see yourself as clearly as my client did and avoid becoming trapped by your schemas and falling into old habits, it's important to develop mindful awareness. You got a taste of this in some of the exercises in the previous chapter. Now we'll focus on further developing this skill. Simply put, mindful awareness means paying attention, or being attuned to your experience and sensations—both external and internal. You intentionally initiate your sensory system and point your awareness wherever you choose. As my friend Laura Fortgang, a talented author and acclaimed professional life coach, describes it, "Being mindful means being aware of everything and certain of nothing." I love this definition because once certainty enters the arena, possibility is eclipsed. The possibility of seeing and feeling through a whole new sensory lens is the harvest of the flexible mind. With awareness and flexibility, you enlist the possibility of seeing with abundant clarity the depth, color, and movement of the world within or around you. For example, consider the ocean. With mindful attention you can hear the sound of the surf with more robust dimensionality. The sensations brought forth by the warm mist and the radiant sun on your face become more pronounced. You can smell and even taste the salt tang of the air. Being fully attuned to your senses allows you to become engaged in a multifaceted experience of the present moment.

The Importance of Practice

Developing a mindfully fit brain requires regular practice. As with anything you choose to learn or master, repetition and intention are necessary. Think about riding a bike or driving a car. Before you were able to take in the scenery, you had to think carefully about the positions of your hands and feet, your posture, steering, speed, and visual cues.

Many years ago, a friend agreed to teach me how to drive a stick shift. He directed me to a street with a very steep incline during peak traffic time. He said that I should tackle the tough stuff right from the start. Though I was already an experienced driver of eight years, I felt my sweaty palms clenching the wheel, my back stiff against the seat, and my eyes darting to the rearview mirror, noting the too-cozy closeness of the vehicle behind me. My heart seemed to pound in time to a staccato but silent refrain: *Left foot engage clutch. Release brake. Accelerate gas pedal with right foot. Gently remove left foot from clutch. Don't wreck your friend's new car.*

Developing this new skill involved intense concentration and effort. Yet only a short time later I found myself driving my newly purchased stick-shift automobile uphill in traffic while listening to the radio, taking in the scenery, and thinking about the midterm exam I was about to take. In that moment, I noticed that I didn't need to focus on the mechanics of the task of driving anymore, at least not with the same degree of intentional concentration as before. Driving stick had now become a memory-accessible, choreographed set of movements. Of course, if you drive your car even a moderate amount, you are enrolled in ongoing practice—practice that reinforces your skill set over and over again.

You might be able to pluck a similar experience from your own memories of building skills. Try this:

1. Call up a memory of the first time you learned something that required your complete focus and attention.

2. See how many of your senses you can engage as you recall that experience: the way it felt, looked, sounded, smelled, and tasted, along with the thoughts and emotions you carried with you at the very beginning.

3. How long was it before you no longer needed to pay such concentrated attention—until there appeared to be an opening for other inputs of awareness?

If your recollection brings you to a memory of artistic or athletic pursuits—tennis, for example—you may be thinking that you could never disengage your intense focus if you want to play well. But see if you can recall the difference between the first time you learned how to make contact with the ball and everything entailed in that and the first time you were able to focus on both hitting the ball and anticipating your opponent's next move.

We've all heard the saying "Practice makes perfect." I don't know about perfect, but practice—the act of doing something over and over, whether with coaching or on your own—is the key to getting information or behaviors to stick to memory. Whether it's practicing your backhand stroke, practicing the piano, or practicing not cowering before an intimidating individual, you are immersed in the intentional act of doing something again and again with several goals in mind:

- Learning new habits

- Unlearning undesirable habits

- Performing well enough or better

- Making all of this stick to memory and perhaps developing a sense of mastery

How Mindfulness Helps You Interact with the Narcissist

In dealing with narcissists, it's important to practice the art of paying attention. For example, if you're mindfully aware of your slumped shoulders as you move with resignation toward another interaction with the narcissist, you're more likely to be able to engage the possibility of positive change. You might notice that your posture arises from a well-worn habit, your mind anticipating the usual defeat. From this moment of clarity, you choose to adopt a chin-up, shoulders-back position of strength and confidence and also angle your awareness toward the other person's face, hands, and physical being, reminding yourself that he is just another member of the fascinating and imperfect human species. With your body and mind well attuned, and with a more realistic assessment of the situation, you are unburdened of the shoulds, the musts, and the schemas. You not only know that you're okay, you can feel it.

Awareness fosters discovery, which in turn fosters freedom. And with that freedom comes the possibility of being responsible for how you show up in the world. Instead of showing the narcissist your guilt-ridden, subjugated, or powerless self as usual, you can be anchored in your authentic, healthy, and grown-up self. Armed with the ownership of your present moment and connected with a sense of empathy for the narcissist's underlying shame and defectiveness, which he clumsily works so hard to mask, you'll have the confidence to tactfully confront him when he crosses the line. By awakening to your automatic reactions, you can recognize several important things:

- Sudden discomfort may be a sign of schema activation.

- The thoughts and feelings activated by your memories may not have any bearing on the present situation.

- You have choices in the present moment.

- You have nothing to prove and no need to hide.

- You have rights too.

As you develop a mindfully polished brain, you can flex your thoughts, beliefs, and predictions like muscles honed by a commitment to careful training and exercise. And just as in developing muscles, becoming grounded in the present moment requires regular practice, even if it's sometimes accompanied by pain. With so much to gain from developing mindfulness, you're probably eager to get started. The following exercise details a simple practice for keeping your mind attuned.

Exercise: Engaging Your Mindful Brain

As discussed, practice is crucial to developing new skills. Make a commitment to carve out five minutes for yourself twice a day to engage in the following practice. For a printable version of this exercise that you can carry with you, go to www.newharbinger.com/27602, (See back of book for more information.) Of course, adding more time to each practice will make your experience more robust and will help to lock in your newly developed awareness skills. You need not seek out a quiet place; you can do this practice almost anywhere. It is, however, important to practice during a period when you aren't likely to be interrupted by someone talking to you.

You can practice with your eyes open or closed. Closing your eyes promotes a deeper and more profound rendezvous with your senses, but keeping them open if you need to is also fine. Read through the instructions several times to familiarize yourself with the process. You might want to make a recording of the instructions to use until your mindfulness practice becomes second nature. As you practice, engage all of your senses.

1. Direct your attention to your breath, and without forcing anything, just maintain the natural pace of your breath and focus on each of the following aspects in turn:

   - With the first breath, notice the rise and fall of your abdomen.

   - With the second breath, tune in to the expansion and contraction of your lungs.

   - With the third breath, feel the cool air coming through your nostrils as you breathe in, and sense the warmth of the air you exhale.

2. Repeat the above process three times, noticing the rise and fall of your abdomen, your lungs expanding and contracting, and the temperature of the air as you inhale and exhale.

3. If your eyes are open, visually notice the space you're occupying. If they're closed, conjure up a memory of the picture. Label what you see: the color, size, shape, dimension, and movement of whatever surrounds you.

4. Notice the sounds in your environment. Allow them to enter your auditory awareness precisely and without judgment. Label each one, from the roaring lyrics of the lawnmower pressing through your window to the rambling medley of children's voices in play and even to the most subtle sounds: the whistle of the air ventilation duct, the tiny tick of the clock, or the faint hum coming from your laptop sitting on your desk.

5. Invite your nasal passages to join you in your practice, making sense out of scents in the air.

6. Point the needle of your compass of awareness to your tongue. As you take a slow breath in and then release it slowly, notice and label any tastes that have taken refuge in your mouth.

7. Direct your attention toward the sensations of anything that you are physically in contact with. Notice your clothing against your skin, a breeze brushing your face, the texture of the surface or firmness of the cushion you're sitting on, the feeling of the ground beneath your feet or the sand between your toes.

8. Turn your attention to your internal world, the world beneath the surface of your skin. If possible, engage in a few simple stretches accompanied by nice, full breaths. Starting with the crown of your head, slowly scan your entire body from top to bottom, including your face, neck, limbs, fingers, and toes. Take notice of sensations in your muscles and viscera: energy, fatigue, tightness, tingling, soreness, numbness, strength, queasiness, or weakness, for example. Just notice. Be aware of emotional responses emerging within. You may notice that your inner sensations emit a resonance of sadness, fear, or anger. Just notice this, label it, and allow your attention to rest upon it quietly, observing without appraisal.

Try to maintain a stance of openness and equanimity, meaning that you ask yourself to do this practice without predictions or predilections crowding your mind. Your thoughts *will* try to seduce you away from your practice. When that happens, just notice them, label them, acknowledge them, and let them move on. If thoughts like *This is foolish. How could this possibly make a difference?* leak in, simply notice that you're having a thought and that this thought is a judgment. Tell yourself, *Okay, I got it*, then let it go and return to your practice.

If schema-driven thoughts invade (for example, *Nothing will ever help me get my needs met; I'm destined to be emotionally lonely and unfulfilled*), use the process of observing, assessing, identifying, and differentiating described in chapter 4. Observe that you're having a familiar thought and assess whether it might relate to an old life theme or schema. If so, identify or label it and acknowledge your understanding of where it comes from. (For example, *Okay, I got it. I know this is my emotional deprivation schema that causes me to feel the sad and lonely little girl in me who didn't get the affection and empathy she needed. It makes me feel like I'll never get my needs met.*) Differentiate it by saying, *But that was then, and this is now.* Then let it go and return to your practice.

Some thoughts, especially those associated with schemas, can be stubborn and unremitting. Your breath is your grounding point. It gently returns you to your practice when you become swept away by the undertow of your thoughts. When you find yourself highly distracted, return your attention to your breathing in the manner described at the start of the exercise, noticing the rise and fall of your abdomen, your lungs expanding and contracting, and the temperature of the air as you inhale and exhale.

The Rewards of Mindfulness

Creating a practice of intentional awareness and discovery can unwrap many beautiful gifts for you to behold and cherish. It also reveals the undesirable ones. Remember, memories are stored in the brain and in the body, and they can be released by any of an infinite number of sensory stimuli. Fortunately, as your awareness becomes more well-attuned and conscious, you can readily discern between truth and fiction and between that which is old and that which is now. This is exactly what you need for taking on the most difficult people in your life with aplomb.

In his continuing effort to illuminate and communicate the majesty of the brain, Dan Siegel explains that, in an attentive state, the brain is capable of reflective awareness, allowing you to differentiate your feelings, thoughts, and sensations and also integrate them within the whole of your mind and body. Without mindful attention, you operate out of the default state of automatic mental activity. The brain is reactive, not necessarily receptive (Siegel 2007).

However, as mentioned earlier, it isn't possible to be in a state of attentive awareness all the time, especially given our makeup and the busy lives we lead. To be perfectly conscious all the time would disable our necessary automatic functionality. Paying attention is a choice and a discipline. Just as paying attention to the condition of your body through conscious eating and exercise may reward you with good health, greater energy, and longevity, paying attention, on purpose, to your thoughts, feelings, and sensations potentially rewards you with a built-in wake-up call, alerting you to delightful moments worth capturing—and obtrusive distortions worth discarding, especially when dealing with the narcissist in your life.

The Four Most Common Masks of the Narcissist and How to Deal with Them

Now that you have an understanding of narcissism, a custom profile of the narcissist in your life, a well-developed inventory of your own schemas and coping styles, and greater mastery of your attentive and flexible brain, you're ready to move on to specific strategies for dealing with the four masks you're most likely to face when dealing with the narcissist in your life: the show-off, the bully, the entitled one, and the addictive self-soother.

The Show-Off

When dealing with the show-off, recognize that you're in the company of someone who hungers for the adoration and envy of others. She may be overtly boastful or covertly charming and self-effacing. She suffers from a sense of invalidity and undesirability but may not be aware of it. She's learned that if she can impress you, she can temporarily nourish her hunger and extinguish her shame.

She finds her reflection in your applause. She appears to have little interest in you apart from the praise and admiration you offer.

With your steady grasp of the present moment, proceed to ignore her obvious solicitations and instead offer positive feedback for the simple and ordinary niceties of the interaction. For example, let's say the narcissist is your friend Vanessa. Instead of saying, as you usually do, "Oh, Vanessa, I just don't know how you do it all. What an exceptional woman you are," you could place your emphasis on everyday things: "Vanessa, I appreciate that you made this lunch date for us. It's nice to be remembered." Focus on thoughtful, unadorned kindnesses instead of the extraordinary, supremely glossy images and actions she presents for your admiration. Even amidst her outstanding achievements in volunteerism and fashion supremacy, you might ferret out a sliver of ordinariness and grant it some honest but modest recognition.

Say she's just been asked to chair the hospital's annual fundraising gala. It's the who's who of community service and a social extravaganza. Following her blow-by-blow account of how they invited her to chair based on her upstanding reputation, poise, and exemplary public relations skills, you could respond with "How nice for you, Vanessa, to be a part of something that will help those who will benefit from the donations to the hospital. Good luck with it."

You candidly and competently steer clear of the traps set by your schemas and don't allow yourself to be blinded by the glare of her 14-karat ego. And while you unwaveringly bask in your own clarity, know that your frank responses might even reach the part of Vanessa that actually longs to be accepted without the burden of grandiloquently proving herself.

The Bully

When dealing with the bully, recognize that you're in the company of someone who has a rigid mistrust of people and their motives. He's fearful that others will try to control him, make a fool of him, or take advantage of him. He believes that no one could truly care about him, given his history of emotional voids and his deep sense of shame and inadequacy. He protects himself by being critical and controlling of others. In order to achieve his craved sense of importance and authority, he must ensure that you feel weak, powerless, and perhaps even stupid.

With your steady grasp of the present moment and newly acquired insights, you are poised with confidence. You look the bully in the eye and carefully proceed to let him know how his words and actions make you feel. For example, let's say that the narcissist is Brad, a colleague who's upset about a project you've just submitted. You might say, "You know, Brad, it's very difficult and, frankly, unacceptable when you speak to me in that tone of voice, criticizing my work because it doesn't measure up to your expectations. I can appreciate that you're disappointed and even frustrated, and I may not like it, but I can accept that if it's true. However, you don't have to be mean about it. I don't think you intend to hurt me, but you sometimes have a way of coming across as overly critical. Not only is it upsetting, it simply isn't very helpful."

Or let's say that the narcissist is Joe, your significant other, who just slipped into bully mode due to a perceived lack of attention from you at a social gathering. You might say, "Joe, I care about how you feel, and I certainly don't want to cause you to feel ignored by me. I can understand that you may get upset when I'm distracted and that you'd like me to be more attentive. It's your responsibility t, not curse at me or call me names. I can't care about elings when you do this. It isn't helpful to us, and it eptable to me."

hese scenarios, you've bypassed your former inclina-in, apologize, counterattack, or run away and cry.

Wrapped in the comforting embrace of your sturdy inner advocate, you're clothed in courage and integrity.

The Entitled One

When dealing with the entitled one, recognize that you're dealing with someone who feels that she can make up her own set of rules and that she should be able to have whatever she wants when she wants it. She behaves as if she is superior and feels that she deserves to be treated differently. She doesn't subscribe to the sentiment of give-and-take. She has trouble being on the receiving end of the word "no" and never appears to feel any remorse for her often pushy and demanding actions. She isn't interested in the feelings of others and can't appreciate or comprehend the value of empathy.

With your steady grasp of the present moment, you gently emerge from the heat rising in your face, take a breath, steady your nerves, and proceed to let her know the real deal. For example, let's say the narcissist is your friend Leanne, who's joining you for dinner. In her usual fashion, she arrived thirty-five minutes late without calling to let you know. The restaurant has a policy that you can't be seated until the entire party has arrived, so you've been waiting at the bar, watching the tables fill. Leanne struts in with no apology and no explanation, and when she's told that it will be a while before the two of you can be seated, she angrily expresses her utter annoyance to the manager regarding this "ludicrous" policy. You are embarrassed by the loud and self-righteous scene she's making and upset by her total lack of respect for you and the value of your time.

This isn't the first time you've found yourself wishing to be invisible during one of Leanne's predictable, entitled tirades. Your typical stance has been to stand back and smile shyly and apologetically for her rude and embarrassing behavior. That would be followed by a roll of your eyes and the thought *Oh well, this is who she is.* But this time you call her aside and say, "Leanne, this is uncomfortable and embarrassing. It's also disappointing that you don't seem to have much regard for my feelings and act as if it's perfectly okay to do as you please, even when it has a negative impact on me. I know that you're accustomed to taking charge and making things go your way, and you take pride in that. It's great to have that kind of savvy in certain situations. But it isn't okay for you to dismiss my rights and my feelings. I know that you may be too upset to talk about this right now, and I suggest that we postpone our dinner. I'm open to talking about this after you've had a chance to calm down."

Bravo. No cowering, no making excuses for her, no letting her off the hook one more time.

The Addictive Self-Soother

When dealing with the addictive self-soother, recognize that you're with someone who is in a state of unknowing avoidance. The intolerable discomfort associated with his unrecognized loneliness, shame, and disconnection when the spotlight isn't casting its shimmering glow upon him sends him hiding beneath the floorboards once again. He may be engrossed in workaholism, drinking binges, spending marathons, or voracious Internet surfing. He may indulge in the delivery of yet another tiring oration on some esoteric or controversial subject, not necessarily because he's seeking attention, but in an effort to avoid feeling the throbbing pulse of his aloneness and fragility. You may go knocking, but he doesn't come out. He can't risk being seen au naturel, with all of his emotions, needs, and longings revealed. You're expected to pander to his selective emotional departures and not request his presence, regardless of the emotional costs to you.

With your steady grasp of the present moment, you remind yourself that he doesn't don this mask on purpose, and that it isn't your fault that he's frequently detached. You act with a sense of responsibility for yourself and your role in the relationship, especially if this is a meaningful relationship. For example, let's say the narcissist is your husband, Al, and he's deeply entrenched in one of his workaholic episodes. You proceed to thoughtfully confront him, saying, "I know how important your work is to you, Al, and I appreciate how your ambition and dedication have provided us with financial security and lovely opportunities. But I miss you, and I'm concerned that you might be pushing harder than necessary. It's difficult for me to sit back and watch without sharing my concern and sense of loss with you. I'd like to talk about it and see if we can come up with a compromise. Please don't dismiss me or say that I just don't get it. This is really important to me. If we can't come up with a solution that satisfies both of our needs, I want to seek professional help."

No longer tossing in the towel or apologizing for your supposed ignorance on the subject of his career, you firmly but thoughtfully reach in to pull him from the darkness of the lonely place he inhabits.

Conclusion

Greetings, you are awake and in attendance. You are empowered with literacy in a newly developed language of emotions, sensations, and thoughts. You can see how important mindful awareness is in your journey to becoming as effective as you can be, especially when dealing with you know who.

Jumping ahead, chapter 7 will show you what can happen when you inform your heightened awareness with a thorough understanding of the geography of the narcissist's brain. You'll learn how to confront the narcissist with empathy while also keeping him on the hook. In many cases, this is a reasonable approach. But narcissists present themselves along a spectrum. Some are merely annoying, while others are truly perilous and perhaps beyond your capacity to influence. With the latter, your newly developed mindful awareness may help you see that the relationship is too damaging to sustain. Therefore, chapter 6 takes a look at severe and dangerous issues of narcissism and how you can safely disengage from the relationship.

chaptor 6

Making an Exit: Escaping Perilous Narcissism

I have spread my dreams under your feet;
Tread softly because you tread on my dreams.

— William Butler Yeats

There are certain circumstances where an intimate relationship with a narcissist isn't worth fighting for, even if you have the leverage. The narcissist may even be a threat to your (and your children's) security, safety, and stability. In the vast majority of cases, these perilous narcissists are male. Proposed explanations for the disparity include male temperament and greater tendency toward aggression, learned behaviors from primary male role models, social or cultural reinforcement, and biologically driven inclinations in reacting to stress and frustration when schemas are activated.

Perilous narcissists never offer remorse, and in some cases they show no signs of having a moral compass. In extreme cases, their self-righteous rigidity may even resemble the traits of sociopaths (now given the label "antisocial personality disorder"); this type of narcissist often demonstrates a complete disregard or contempt for others and for intrinsic human experiences. If you find yourself involved with such a narcissist, please consider making a safety plan to protect yourself and create an avenue for departure from the relationship.

Identifying Perilous Narcissism

Here are some characteristic behaviors of perilous narcissists. Read through the following lists and carefully consider whether the narcissist in your life engages in these behaviors. Also consider the frequency and extent to which he displays these behaviors. If the narcissist in your life engages in just a few of these behaviors and only on occasion, it might be possible to salvage the relationship. If, however, these behaviors are frequent and pervasive, and particularly if they involve threats to your safety, it's probably best to seek a way out. If you don't know where to turn for help, contact the National Domestic Violence Hotline at 1-800-799-7233.

Threats to Financial and Legal Security

- Gambles excessively

- Spends excessively

- Won't get a job

- Feels entitled to drink and drive

- Buys, uses, or sells illicit drugs

- Views child pornography

- Visits prostitutes

- Evades taxes

- Engages in corrupt and fraudulent acts

- Steals

Threats to Physical or Emotional Safety

- Engages in physically or verbally abusive behavior

- Threatens to harm you, your children, others, or possibly himself

- Disparages you and your children in public

- Destroys property, throws things, threatens to take the children or leave you penniless, or takes out his aggression on pets

- Insists on driving when under the influence of substances, even with you or your children in the car

Threats to Stability in Relationship and the Community

- Has affairs or engages in other promiscuous or risky sexual behavior, including visiting prostitutes or strip clubs or problematic viewing of pornography or visiting adult chat rooms

- Carelessly exposes children to inappropriate material, language, or behaviors

- Lies pathologically about almost anything

- Gets into brawls with neighbors and other community members

- Doesn't display neighborly conduct despite warnings from authorities, for example, playing loud music, having no regard for the appearance of property, or being noisy or exhibitionistic

In recent years, many female clients have come to me with stories about these kinds of behaviors. They are burdened with sorrow, difficult questions, and fear about the future of their relationship and the consequences for their children. In many cases, within minutes of walking into my office they begin to tearfully talk about multitudes of evidence of their partner's sexual transgressions, from infidelity to compulsive viewing of pornography (sometimes of horrifically violent material) to participation in adult chat rooms to visits to prostitutes and strip club back rooms. Their partners often spend countless hours and thousands of dollars engaging in these sexual behaviors.

Because this profile is so common, and because women often feel significant shame about revealing that their partner engages in such behavior, in this chapter I'll focus on these sexual miscreants. If you're in a relationship with a narcissist who is prone to physically aggressive outbursts or behaviors that threaten your safety, please seek outside assistance immediately. Likewise, if the narcissist's behaviors present a genuine threat to your financial or legal security, I encourage you to develop a plan to protect yourself and your children or extract yourself from the relationship, consulting a professional for help in this if need be.

Excuses, Excuses

Once discovered, the narcissist typically denies wrongdoing or tries to minimize the damage. He's usually quick to offer the excuse that he's just like all men or to blame his partner for being overweight, boring, prudish, or too involved with the children, her job, or others. Keep in mind that his problematic behaviors aren't the only way to deal with a sense of loneliness or sexual frustration. Of course, the narcissist isn't particularly interested in hearing about how his partner feels anyway, much less talking about the issue, examining his behavior, or working on it.

And then there's that assertion that this is just natural male sexuality. For the entitled narcissistic man, who is unable to tolerate feeling isolated or emotionally uncomfortable, this is the perfect rationalization. How convenient to be a member of a species in which he is conferred the absolute right to engage in sexual activity beyond his relationship. How convenient to claim he has no say when it comes to the demands of his phallic emperor. (And how strange that the sole exception to his all-encompassing supremacy is being held hostage to a fragment of his anatomy.) But consider this: If that were true, if his damaging sexual behaviors were just part of the male human condition, then why does he engage in them in secrecy, and why does he respond with denial and blaming others when found out?

That said, nature does play a role in holding men's brains hostage once they've entered this sexual territory. Writer and philosopher Roger Scruton points out that once people are led by their porn addiction "to see sex in the instrumentalized way that pornography encourages, they begin to lose confidence in their ability to enjoy sex in any other way than through fantasy" (2010, 157).

The brain can be hijacked by sexual stimulation, much like it responds to sugar. Some of the data on brain function suggests that the addictive and stimulating rush of pleasure from pornography and other sexual activities outside of a partnership can overshadow the pleasure once found in the endorphin-releasing satisfaction of a sexual interlude with one's partner. This feeds into the coping style of the narcissist, who has a chronic need to shut out his deeply rooted pangs of loneliness and emptiness—experiences he may see as boredom. His search for detached self-stimulation when not engaged in other distractions or holding court can lead him to seek out quick highs that eventually may become enduring addictions, including sex addictions. But this ravenous desire for stimulation is a distraction from the underlying (and intolerable) emotional hunger he feels and that remains unnourished.

It doesn't hurt that so much of the easily accessible world of Internet pornography, phone sex lines, and the like is designed to stroke the male ego, putting the narcissist on the pedestal where he feels he belongs. Plus, sexual encounters via pornography or with prostitutes require no intimacy, allowing the narcissist to get a quick fix with no reciprocity required. Given that narcissists aren't very good at giving back, how convenient that there are no expectations placed upon him, no one he must talk to or interact with authentically, and no one else's needs to consider. Even better, the object of his fantasy often pretends to find him absolutely irresistible and acts highly aroused and excited by his "sexual prowess" and the size of his bulging…wallet. What an enticing feast for the insatiable approval seeker.

Drawing the Line

As damaging as these behaviors are, not all narcissists who engage in them fall into the category of perilous narcissists, so it's important to determine where your narcissist lies on the spectrum. When the secret activities of a moderate narcissist are discovered, his response is likely to quickly evolve from floundering and fumbling to angry and blaming and ultimately to dismissing your ridiculousness at being so bothered by his "boys will be boys" behavior. The mighty stud feels justified and entitled to do what "all men do."

Though the perilous narcissist will react in a similar way, he will exhibit more intense anger and volatility, unremitting remorselessness, lack of shame, and unwillingness to change. He may also become aggressive or engage in increasingly aggressive sexual behavior with you. On the other hand, he may show a complete absence of sexual interest.

Deciding Whether to Stay or Go

In the case of perilous narcissism, safety should be your first and foremost priority, especially if the narcissist's volatility, violence, or threats are increasing; if he is persistent and unremorseful in perpetrating verbal or emotional abuse; or if he responds to your upset contemptuously or hatefully, beyond his chronic disrespect and maltreatment of you.

Many women describe these perilous behaviors as the most heartbreaking and horrifying events in their relationship. Even if they use the most thoughtful phraseology and kindest tone of voice in advocating for peace for themselves and for the sake of the children, the perilous narcissist may only become more callous and menacing. Again, this is a signal to put your safety first and come up with an exit strategy. But because so many narcissists can continue to don the Prince Charming mask even in these most difficult times, it can be difficult to assess just how entrenched their perilous behaviors are. The following case example provides some insight into how the perilous narcissist can twist the truth in an attempt to absolve himself of highly egregious transgressions.

• *Samantha and Todd's Story*

Samantha and Todd have been married for eighteen years. They have two children in grade school. After years of kowtowing to her husband's supersized ego, Samantha discovers that Todd has been regularly viewing Internet pornography and visiting adult chat rooms. His first response is denial, but Samantha shows him evidence she's found indicating a long-standing habit. Todd shifts to defense, shouting, "So what! It's what all men do. What's the big deal?" For a change, Samantha doesn't back down. She demands an explanation and says that she won't tolerate this behavior. Perilous narcissism begins to reveal itself as Todd gets enraged. Towering over her, fists clenched, he says, "Trust me, Samantha, you don't want to keep pushing me!"

Yet Samantha somehow manages to maintain her courage and again demands an explanation, and also expresses how hurt and betrayed she feels. Not surprisingly, Todd displaces the responsibility, cruelly and unfairly pointing the finger at Samantha: "Maybe if you weren't such a nag… Maybe if you paid more attention to your fat body and cared about our sex life, I wouldn't be looking at porn!"

Crushed, Samantha stares at him incredulously and begins to cry. Todd gets in her face and sneers, "I'm not falling for the tears, Sam. You'd better get a grip! This is your issue. Stop being such a prude and get yourself some serious help. You're nuts! You'll be sorry if you keep pushing me!" Samantha, fighting to feel "felt" by Todd, is awash in anger and pain, so she confronts him again, demanding that he explain himself and promise that he'll stop.

But Todd remains remorseless and impervious and declares, "I'm done with this crap and with you!" Kicking over a chair and throwing a coffee cup into the sink, where it breaks into pieces, he walks out of the house and slams the door.

Samantha drops to the floor, alone, devastated, and sobbing into her hands. In the next room, the kids have heard everything. They sit paralyzed on the floor, huddled together and crying.

Eventually Todd returns. A silent and uneasy truce reigns. At first, Samantha's fears of being alone, of facing Todd's vengeance if she seeks divorce, and of the possibility that Todd might receive joint custody of the children make her feel paralyzed. A nauseated feeling of futility and helplessness constantly twists in her gut. But Samantha has learned something important about Todd, and she uses it to build her resolve. As the weeks and months pass, she discreetly seeks legal advice. With the support of friends, family, and therapy to strengthen her will and confidence, Samantha enters the dreaded legal battle with Todd.

After the divorce, some aspects of life are more challenging. Todd often fails to maintain the visitation schedule because it "interferes with his work" or, more likely, his new party-boy lifestyle. When the kids do visit, Todd tells them to do whatever they want, as long as they leave him and his computer alone. Afterward, Samantha repairs the damage, letting them know that they are entitled to their hurt and confusion and that their father has problems to deal with, but not bad-mouthing him.

Todd is also predictably late with every alimony and child support payment, so Samantha often has to work overtime. She regrets losing this time with her kids, but she's grateful to have preserved her sanity and safety, and she knows that this is most important for the kids in the long run.

Reforming the Moderate Narcissist

Fortunately, most narcissists don't fall into the perilous category. If you're committed to staying in the relationship for whatever reason, or if you genuinely feel your partner is capable of change, you don't have to put up with continued maltreatment. With professional help, the moderate narcissist usually eventually apologizes and promises to change his behavior. He may even come to understand the impact of his sexual behavior on you, your feelings toward him, and your sexual relationship. But without help, it's unlikely that such changes will occur or endure. Rebuilding trust after a breach like this is a threefold endeavor:

- The offended partner must feel understood.

- The offended partner must figure out and find a way to express what she needs to feel safe—to trust again and reengage in intimacy.

- The offended partner needs to feel safe enough to acknowledge the narcissist's changes and to recognize and appreciate any signs of empathy he shows, whether solicited or unsolicited.

At first glance, it may seem as if those three requirements fall entirely on the shoulders of the betrayed partner. But a closer examination reveals that all three depend on the narcissist's commitment to change.

For you to feel understood, you must sense that your partner gets you—who you are at your core. To do this, he must learn to be empathically attuned. He'll need help—someone to teach him skills to avoid falling into spontaneous defensiveness and quick angry reactions, which help him avoid shameful "bad guy" feelings. Without these skills, he will fail.

Likewise, if you are to feel safe in expressing your needs and rebuilding trust, your partner must find the courage to dive into the dark water and explore the sunken vessel that houses his early experiences. He must be willing to look at how he developed his propensity to engage in addictive self-stimulating, and ultimately self-defeating, behaviors. This is necessary if he is to generously provide, without resentment, the reassurance and transparency necessary for restoring trust. This will also put him in a better position to share with you what led him down this precipitous path, which will be invaluable in preventing backsliding.

The third requirement—acknowledging the narcissist's changes and appreciating any signs of empathy—may seem the most difficult. Doing this can feel like saying, "Everything's better now. You can go back to being as you were." Just remember that your feelings of safety are a necessary prerequisite, and those feelings will only occur if the narcissist makes genuine changes. He must also be patient and realize that your reentry into intimacy with him will be gradual. He must understand that your comfort level will wax and wane, especially when certain stimuli, such as the anniversary of a betrayal, trigger painful emotions. Finally, he must offer verbal reassurances in all of these regards and continue to acknowledge and accept that he is responsible for the rift between you. In time, you may heal and feel securely reattached to your self-worth, allowing you to be vulnerable with him once again—and perhaps eventually integrate reciprocity, generosity, and forgiveness into your relationship.

All of that may seem pretty hard to imagine, and indeed, it is rare. But with motivation, patience, and appropriate leverage, it can occur. I've been privileged to witness this process of transformation as both parties struggled to find their way, making sense out of the conflict, meeting each other's needs, and ultimately creating a relationship that's better, more honest, and more satisfying than it had ever been, even prior to sexual transgressions.

The process of healing isn't fast and brings many painful feelings to the surface: anger, sadness, fear, and grief surrounding a stained chapter in a shared life story. Couples engaged in this process often ask how they can deal with the ugly reality of this part of their relationship. Once they move beyond the acute phase of disbelief, anger, and anguish and have agreed upon a plan for safety and trust, I ask them to imagine a beautiful architectural structure. I point out that what usually makes such structures pleasingly eye-catching isn't perfectly laid brick, one-dimensional color, or highly polished stone, but imperfections: bruises in the brick, a medley of colors, or weathered, rough-edged stones. The collective and its contrasts are what make for rich and beautiful architecture. These structures have stood the test of time, of natural forces, and perhaps of war, and they have also been cared for by people who cherish them. This is an apt metaphor for an enduring relationship: sturdy despite the challenges to its foundation, rich with colors that depict both the brilliance and the sorrow, with some imperfections that lend character, and, most of all, painstakingly cared for by those who want it to last.

If you and the narcissist have children, love and concern for them can be a tremendous motivator for working hard to mend broken trust and address the damage narcissism has wrought in your relationship. Unfortunately, out of their desperate need to feel safe, children often assume the position of marital arbiters. Don't put them in this position or allow them to function in this way. And as you learned in earlier chapters, the effects of narcissistic anger, entitlement, and disparagement on children can be quite damaging. Many children mimic a narcissistic parent's actions and internalize that parent's style of thinking and interacting. Alternatively, children may take on problematic traits and coping styles of a nonnarcissistic parent who is passive, self-sacrificing, or fails to provide protection.

Conclusion

If you're in a relationship with a perilous narcissist, I cannot over-emphasize the importance of assuring your own safety and that of children, if you have them. That said, the narcissist's prowess in wielding his charm can make it difficult to determine whether he is truly unredeemable. Observe him closely and mindfully—in the moment and not through the filters of your own past experience. If you think you might get through to him and he may be capable of change, use the communication skills in this book to try to engage the wounded, damaged person within. If you have a long-term relationship, this may be worthwhile, as difficult as it may be.

If you elect to stay and try to salvage the relationship, empathy will be one of your most effective tools in fostering change. To that end, chapter 7 outlines a strategy for utilizing empathy while not backing down from ensuring that your own needs are met.

chapter 7

Using Empathic Confrontation: A Winning Strategy for Interpersonal Effectiveness

If we could read the secret history of our enemies, we should find in each man's life sorrow and suffering enough to disarm all hostility.

—Henry Wadsworth Longfellow

Even if you've determined that your narcissist doesn't fall into the perilous category, being in his company when he's in his less-than-charming, Mr. Hyde mode can feel like being with an enemy. Schemas get triggered, leaving you feeling woozy, speechless, or at the end of your rope. These people seem to be able to suck the oxygen right out of the room. Being angry and fed up temporarily thickens your skin to the narcissist's demeaning behavior, or so it seems. But carrying anger around can become exhausting after a while. Before you know it, the fatigue can bring you right back to feeling raw and powerless. So you surrender to the narcissist's offensive maneuvers and wait for him to eventually, hopefully, return to his delightfully charming and generous mode.

However, with your new mindfulness and communication skills, this need not be the dynamic. You can remain sturdier and unwavering in the center of the storm. You need not compromise your values or integrity in the face of the narcissist's demands. The bottom line is that you have rights, valid needs and desires, and inherent value. You're worth sticking up for!

But to further your interpersonal effectiveness and achieve more rewarding outcomes, you'll need more than a fit mind and attuned inner wisdom; you need to truly get who the narcissist is. You need more than an intellectual literacy in his issues and life story; you also need an emotional literacy in his inner world. In other words, you need to feel what his experience of the world is like. It's like feeling his mind inside of yours (something you may not want to do with a perilous narcissist). This isn't mind reading; this is what is known as empathy.

Before you read on, one important note: This approach is inappropriate with anyone who makes you feel unsafe or abused. That calls for a completely different protocol, often requiring exit strategies and safety plans. If the narcissist in your life is violent, abusive, or threatens your safety in any way, please seek assistance immediately. If you don't know where to turn for help, contact the National Domestic Violence Hotline at 1-800-799-7233.

Distinguishing between Empathy and Compassion

There seems to be considerable confusion when it comes to the term "empathy." Many people use it interchangeably with "compassion." And while both may occur in the context of bearing witness to another person's suffering or joy, the two are quite different from one another, and in ways that are highly pertinent in any discussion of narcissism.

Many clients are taken aback when I advocate using empathy in confronting the narcissist. They misinterpret my meaning, thinking I'm asking them to feel sorry for the abrasive bully who has tortured them time and again. So let's take a moment to differentiate empathy from compassion.

Empathy is a capacity to truly *understand* the experience of another, emotionally, mentally, and sometimes even physically. It doesn't mean that you necessarily agree with, condone, or support the other person's feelings and behavior, simply that you understand it in a "felt" way. In an empathic state, you experience the thoughts, feelings, and sensations of another within your own mind and body. It's as if you can feel the person's experience resonating within yourself. You are fully attuned.

Here's an example: Let's say a dear friend and colleague arrives at work visibly shaking and upset. She proceeds to describe a car accident she almost had while driving to work. She can still visualize the truck coming toward her and the split second in which she steered her car toward the shoulder to avoid being hit. She then describes how she stopped to offer help to another motorist who wasn't as lucky and was struck badly. She becomes tearful as she talks about the what-ifs of the situation and how lucky she feels to be alive and safe. Nervously laughing, she says, "Imagine, being so happy to be here at work on a Monday morning." You tell her how happy you are, too, that she's okay. You express that you can only imagine how terrifying it must have been.

You picture the event as she describes it. You capture the scenario in your mind, along with all of the what-ifs. You feel your own body clenching as she describes the sound of horns blaring and the impact of the truck crashing into the other car just a few feet from where she had stopped. You feel your heart rate elevating at the thought of a phone call reporting that your friend had been badly injured or killed. You might even recall the experience of a similar event in your own life. When she says that she'll be okay and just needs a few moments to catch her breath and grab some coffee, you can completely feel her desire to seek a sense of calm and relief; it rises within you too. You get it. This is empathy.

While compassion requires this kind of empathic awareness, or understanding, it goes further. Compassion is a radiating desire to console, comfort, and alleviate the pain and suffering of another. It's rooted in a deep sense of empathic sensing where you have captured a clear felt sense of the other person's experience, followed by sympathy (defined as sorrow in response to your empathic sensing) for the other person's misfortune. Compassion is the tendency to move beyond empathy for another person's aches; it means feeling compelled to extend a kindness, to do something about the person's pain, to bring relief or healing.

Going back to the previous example, with compassion you would hug your friend to comfort her and say something like "Please, let me get the coffee for you. Why don't you just freshen up and then sit down and take a few quiet moments for yourself. I'll cover for you. And let me know if there's anything else I can do, even if you just need to talk." With compassion, it's difficult to walk away without desiring, imagining, or executing some plan or action for relief.

When it comes to utilizing empathy and compassion in your relationship with a narcissist, the challenge can be daunting, given how rarely narcissists expose their vulnerability. Yet the ability to experience empathy and even perhaps compassion for this troubling and troubled person is just the skill you need for achieving more satisfying outcomes in interactions—and hopefully a more satisfying relationship.

Feeling "Felt"

Healthy development of the child into an adult is contingent upon a parent or caregiver providing an attuned emotional connection—in other words, empathy. As a child looks up into her parent's eyes for comfort or approval, the parent consciously reflects back an understanding of her experience, whether joy, fear, confusion, or sorrow. The parent accepts and validates the child's feelings or needs and helps her make sense of what's happening within her: "Of course, sweetie, I know it's very scary to see monsters on your bedroom wall and you don't want to be there all alone with them. Let's go and see if maybe it's just those silly shadows, dancing in the moonlight, that sneaked in again."

When this need for attuned connection isn't adequately met, the child's experience of feeling misunderstood, invisible, meaningless, lonely, or even ashamed of unmet longing for connection can lead to painful self-labels, such as "weak," "foolish," or "unlovable," and self-defeating life patterns, such as detachment, avoidance, or bullying. Feeling that others get you is a highly underestimated human need, and it's crucial for the cultivation of empathic awareness, which is essential for healthy emotional and interpersonal development.

A key aspect of narcissism is attempting to feel visible, but in a maladaptive way. In the absence of feeling "gotten," narcissists search for approval, primarily in regard to their performance. They fight to receive special entitlements as proof of their success and extraordinariness. They also attempt to maintain absolute control and demand emotional autonomy of themselves, deriving a sense of power from not needing anyone. There is a deep well of shame attached to their quashed but very human longing to be understood, visible, loved, and accepted. Their unmet need for attuned emotional connection and their undeveloped understanding of their own narrative leaves them without access to experiences of empathy with others.

Rather than tuning in to others, the narcissist remains caught up in the distracting pursuit of approval: *How am I doing? She really likes me. I think I nailed it. I think I impressed him. I wonder if they like what I just said. Uh-oh, I think I'm in trouble. I'll show them.* This single-minded "all about me" focus prevents the narcissist from truly engaging in interactions, much less experiencing or conveying empathy. As a result, those he interacts with are left feeling lonely, empty, and frustrated.

However, with the exception of people suffering from certain forms of brain injury, almost all humans possess the capacity for empathy. Fostering empathy in a narcissist isn't an impossible mission—but it is challenging. It requires sound professional help from an expert who understands narcissism and is competent in working with this population. Unfortunately, getting narcissists to agree to go to therapy is usually difficult. It takes leverage—establishing meaningful consequences, such as losing someone or something important, and enforcing those consequences if they don't get help.

As stated previously, empathy doesn't necessarily mean agreeing with others or condoning their actions; it simply requires understanding. To this end, we mentally and emotionally conjure up an internal image, story, or bodily sensation that allows us to imagine or feel the experiences or intentions of others. We become emotionally, mentally, and physically engaged in making sense out of what we see and hear, whether it's a character in a movie, a loved one standing before us, or perhaps even the person in the mirror. This lights a path to meaning and unburdens us of misappropriated responsibility, blame, toxic anger, shame, helplessness, and guilt. We must have access to our vulnerable side in order to take in the pain or joy of another. This is often an impasse for the narcissist.

Empathy also creates clarity and a greater awareness of what is real, freeing us from the distorted perceptions imposed by the filters of our schemas. This opens the door to emotional relief from biased beliefs and unnecessary self-defensiveness and clears the path toward personal transformation.

This state of "knowing," of emotional and mental sensibility, provides much-needed balance when dealing with a narcissist. His ways of behaving and relating have so much power to bring up old, schema-driven beliefs and feelings that can make you doubt the truth about who you are, your worth, and perhaps even your capacity to be in a relationship. You may lose your courage to express your opinions or feel ashamed or less-than if your ideas aren't as "bold" or "clever" as his. Because empathy allows you to deeply understand who the narcissist is and why he is that way, it's the perfect antidote, fortifying you to stand your ground, hold him accountable, and not take responsibility for his issues. Best of all, you can show up in interactions with him without the burden of exhausting anger, defensiveness, or submissiveness. You get him. You may even feel badly for him and might even tell him that, but you can do so without giving in and without giving up your rights.

With time, your empathy—your felt sense of the narcissist's suffering—may even deepen into compassion. This doesn't always happen, and of course it depends upon how shattered your heart has become, weathering the harsh and inclement storms of narcissism. If the damage isn't too great, you may find yourself wanting to help, comfort, accept, or even forgive. Sometimes this is perfectly appropriate; it might even be what's necessary—as long as it doesn't violate your fundamental and nonnegotiable rights and needs.

A Brief Look at the Science of Empathy

In the 1980s and 1990s, neuroscientists discovered an intriguing type of neurons that are activated both when we perform a certain action, such as grasping a cup or a fork, or even smiling or frowning, and when we observe someone else performing the same action (Iacoboni 2009). It's almost like the brain is responding as if we are viewing our own reflection in a mirror. Therefore these brain cells are called mirror neurons.

Recent neuroscience investigations into empathy utilizing patterns observed in functional magnetic resonance imaging scans suggest that context and individual makeup, including biology, personality traits, and emotional states, play a role in understanding the degree to which an individual can access empathic awareness.

Apparently, connecting and attuned responses (prosocial responses) are sometimes overshadowed by the motivation to seek revenge or punish, especially when perceptions of unfairness or intentional harm are present.

What does this tell us about the narcissist? Perhaps his need to protect himself is keeping him walled off from painfully disturbing emotions, especially those that make him feel as though he isn't meeting your needs. When you tearfully express your pain and loneliness, his annoyance, schemas, and locked-down emotional state keep him virtually blindfolded. Unable to see and sense your feelings, he is spared from sensing his own vulnerability. Instead, he instantaneously flips into a self-righteous mode of angry sighs and dismissive retorts. You may even find yourself on the receiving end of a retaliating response that arises from his sense that you're intentionally trying to make him feel bad about himself.

• *Sue and Don's Story*

Don has just learned from his stepsister that his father is dying. His lifelong distressful relationship with that demanding, never-satisfied man who never once told him he loved him is coming to an end. Don's wife, Sue, watches as Don harrumphs into the phone, looking annoyed and rolling his eyes even as his stepsister expresses sadness and her sympathy for him.

For years, Sue has observed Don's coldness whenever anyone, herself included, shared a caring or concerned emotion with him. She used to feel annoyed and sometimes hurt by Don's coldness, but she's come to realize that this is Don's issue, not hers, and that in this moment her husband is making a fierce effort to not feel the intolerable pain of having to let go of the fantasy of a father who might come to his senses one day and tell Don that he always loved him and was proud of him. Sue knows that Don won't be able to acknowledge this fantasy or accept the reality of his loss without professional help; he finds it too shameful to admit that he needs his dad—or anyone, for that matter.

Sue sees the look on his face, hears his dismissive grunt, and recognizes a familiar pattern. She also empathically senses a resonance with her own feelings, recalling the not-infrequent times in her childhood when her dad would get home late at night extremely drunk. She recalls how he would storm into her room, waking her and yelling at her for some minor or imagined infraction. Her mother, in the neighboring bedroom, silently waited her turn to be admonished for her imperfection du jour. With no one to protect her, Sue had to be strong, fighting back fright and burning tears as she heard her dad yelling and throwing things in the next room. Once the chaos died down, Sue's older sister would tiptoe into her room and remind her that she just needed to be quiet and be a good girl. She told her not to worry, "The sun will come out tomorrow." Sue remembers her own inner harrumphing when her sister left the room: *Who cares? Nothing will ever change! No, no, wait. I'll try harder. I will. I promise.*

Even though her personal experience was quite different from Don's, it created a resonance that allowed Sue to get the look on her husband's face and understand his desire to push away any unearthing of the fear and hurt buried within. His tone, posture, gestures, and facial expression informed her with a sensory understanding of his stoic sense of entrapment. And although she felt a desire to comfort Don, she knew that he would resist and didn't take that personally. She had done a lot of work on herself and had come to realize that emotional release wasn't a sign of being foolish, overly sentimental, or ignorant, as Don had so often said when she expressed her feelings, fears, and vulnerability.

Sue had also succeeded in getting Don to quit making those derogatory statements. With courage, patience, and empathy, she had helped him see the origins of his behavior in all of those years of living with a demanding and depriving dad. She had also pointedly disconnected from interactions anytime Don heaped demeaning labels on her. Still, he continued to flamboyantly express his discomfort in nonverbal terms. Because Sue now understood that this wasn't about her and could link Don's emotions to her own painful early experiences, she actually found his expressions useful, as they revealed, in a felt way, that Don was struggling. As always, Don attempted to hide his struggle deep within his impermeable, protective walls. Because he had chosen to steer clear of any self-examination or therapy, he remained a prisoner of his memories and an obedient servant to his coping method of being tough and independent and dutifully attempting to conceal all upsetting emotions.

Yet Don's desire to stuff his emotions was like trying to silence a toddler who wants your attention when you're on the phone. Tugging and crying, the child wails unrelentingly until you take notice of him and his upset. As a parent, you have some options: You could attempt to force him to be silent with intimidation or threats, and that might be successful after several attempts. Unfortunately, the result is a child who sinks into a withered state of surrender, stuffing his distress. Alternatively, you might gather the child on your lap to soothe him while you continue your conversation. Or, if he's truly in great distress, you might hang up and lovingly attend to him.

Don, who was on the receiving end of the first type of parenting response, learned early on how to stuff his feelings and self-soothe with distractions. Now, as an adult, he engages in a variety of self-soothing behaviors like drinking too much, spending countless hours surfing the Web, and buying far too many electronics and technical gadgets, all in an attempt to silence his "nagging" emotions and stuff them into submission.

Sue has a keen empathy for Don's reactions and responses even though she doesn't like them and doesn't find them helpful to their relationship. In fact, these behaviors are damaging their intimate, sexual life. Because Don lacks empathy, not just for Sue, but also for himself, his destructive and detached coping habits remain entrenched. The walls he erects make Sue feel more and more shut out, and she finds it difficult to be drawn to him when he offers a playful invitation for a sexual interlude. Of course, Don feels shut out when Sue rejects his advances, so he rolls his eyes, grunts, and turns away, perpetuating and deepening the pattern. This situation can't be resolved until Don develops some empathy for the impact of his detachment on Sue and appreciates the loneliness she feels. His lack of awareness isn't for lack of effort on Sue's part. Countless times she's tried to tell Don that she feels locked out and alone and simply can't switch into an excited and spontaneous sexual mode in the absence of emotional intimacy, affection, and playfulness. She needs to know him and sense that he knows her.

Mirroring the Other

Shared human experiences are opportunities for new wisdom, and wisdom provides a gateway to freedom from false beliefs, distractions, and self-defeating behaviors. Once our mental vision is clear, we can see and sense the strengths and struggles others experience. When this clarity and attendant empathy emerge in a relationship, people become mirrors for one another. We all thrive on seeing an accurate representation of ourselves reflected and held in the mind and heart of a significant other, even when we don't share the same point of view. We all want to feel understood—not judged, ignored, or belittled—for who we are and how we experience and respond to the world, even if it may seem silly sometimes. This is what builds a foundation that's strong enough to withstand the weighty and painful triggers that we always face in our most important relationships.

For example, consider what might happen if Don makes a sexual advance and Sue responds, "I'm sorry, but I'm not interested right now. I know this upsets you, but it's difficult for me to feel aroused when I've felt so alone for so long. When you stay locked away in your own world, I feel completely shut out and disconnected from you. I wish I felt more included. When I don't have any sense of how you're feeling or what you're thinking, it gets really lonely for me."

The likely result is that Don will hear this through his defectiveness filter as *You're an asshole who only thinks of yourself, and you're a failure as a partner.* But what if instead he could empathically sense Sue's struggle and bypass the distractions of triggered feelings of inadequacy and helplessness? That might open the door to a different response: "Sue, I know. I get it. When I'm cut off and distant, it makes you feel very alone, and that makes it hard to feel close to me sexually. I know that it's really important to you that I share more of my feelings and show more interest in you. I know that we deal with being upset very differently, and it doesn't work well for you, or for us, when I shut down. I may not always get it, but I can sense that struggle in you and it makes even more sense when I'm aware of it. I know how much pain you've already endured with your dad, who was supposed to be there for you."

I know you're probably thinking, *Yeah, right... The narcissist in my life would never respond that way.* The fact is, you're probably right; it's extremely unlikely without professional help or meaningful leverage that captures the narcissist's attention because he'll face consequences if he doesn't make a sincere effort to address the issue. Unfortunately, even with professional help, this kind of transformation may be impossible. All too often, narcissists' relationships end up encrusted in an eroded, decaying framework that simply cannot be repaired.

But if hope still abides and the narcissist commits to therapy or self-examination, you may be wondering how to express your appreciation while also maintaining sufficient leverage that he won't assume everything is better and drop out of treatment prematurely. The solution is to find a balanced approach where you celebrate the little victories of budding awareness and changes in behavior in a direct way, perhaps saying something like "I can see that you're making an effort to be more considerate of my feelings and opinions. [Offer a specific example here.] I appreciate that, and it makes me feel closer to you. But I'm not sure how to share this with you without making it sound like everything is okay. I don't want to ignore what you're doing, but I also don't want to give the impression that everything is fine. I need to know that you get that and can understand my dilemma."

Under His Skin

Brace yourself! Here comes the *real* challenge. Many of my clients who are dealing with a narcissist have heard me say, "You must light the torch and lead the way in order for change to occur," meaning they must extend empathy in order to receive it. However, I also affirm that they shouldn't have to carry that torch indefinitely; the narcissist must reciprocate and become receptive. Throughout, you must carefully measure and evaluate progress and decide if enough is enough. You always have the right to change your mind and make a different choice.

I know—it's a tall order. But think about it: If the narcissist is someone who plays a significant role in your life, it may be worthwhile to try to make it work, or to assure yourself that you've done all you could before calling it quits. And now that you've chosen to peruse the biography and autobiography aisle of your emotional library, rather than the schema-driven fiction aisle, you can better understand the makeup of both the narcissist and yourself and remain judiciously grounded in truth.

Putting yourself in the narcissist's shoes means trying to sense and genuinely feel his inner world. Specific techniques can help you do this. For example, when the narcissist begins to address you sharply, you could superimpose the face of a lonely and unloved little boy over that of the grown man before you. As you picture the face of that child, try to imagine his experience: his painful feelings, his sense of defectiveness and shame, his loneliness and emotional emptiness, the impossible but inescapable conditions he had to meet to gain attention, love, or approval—perhaps sometimes confusingly mixed with the message that he was the best, greatest, and most perfect boy in the world. You summon up your empathy and embrace the boy that the man before you cannot bear to consciously feel.

This brilliant strategy was a gift from my dear friend, Dr. Jeffrey Young, when I was learning how to—in a limited way—reparent clients with issues of narcissism. When reparenting the narcissist, emphasis is placed upon nurturing the lonely and deprived child hidden within, doing so with both caring and guidance. Limited reparenting includes empathy and setting limits, experiences the narcissist didn't have as a child, modeling ways he can nurture and care for this part of himself. This heals damaging schemas and reorganizes the way the child is cradled in memory.

You'll find that summoning up empathy and possibly even compassion for the child within the narcissist is an extremely helpful tool for maintaining an even keel when he starts to tip the boat. Try to capture and firmly hold a snapshot of the vulnerable child within your mind's eye while the adult before you is once again carelessly sputtering about one thing or another. This will fill you with the knowledge that what typically drives his drama is a need to avoid the feelings of the little guy behind the scenes—the vulnerability he regards as pathetic and inadequate. You can look upon and experience that child as simply frightened, sad, and deprived, even if he was sometimes spoiled too.

There is a beautiful line in William Wordsworth's lyrical poem "My Heart Leaps Up" where he says, "The Child Is father of the Man" (1892, 200). Perhaps he was talking about the voice of the inner child presiding over the mind of the grown man, just like a schema or an outdated template for living. Without a discerning awareness, the adult narcissist is taking his cues from the child within—the child with the vast collection of painful early experiences that haunt his interpersonal relationships in the here and now.

Here's a helpful tip: Try to obtain a photograph of the narcissist as a child. This can be very useful in building empathy or compassion. It's also a good idea to have a photo of you as a child to remind you that the vulnerable part within you also needs your compassion and care. Some of my clients have their pictures laminated and keep them at hand to use as a visual cue during this phase of change.

Keeping the Narcissist on the Hook

Filling your emotional reservoir with empathy and compassion doesn't mean letting the narcissist off the hook when he's behaving badly. While it is necessary to harness your understanding and emotional generosity, it's equally necessary to hold the narcissist accountable when he acts condescending, selfish, controlling, or downright mean. Essentially, you want to aim for confrontation from an empathic stance. The following five vignettes will illustrate how to use empathic confrontation with the narcissist in your life. Feel free to recast the narcissist as a friend, spouse, boss, colleague, sibling, or other family member as relevant to your situation. Each scenario focuses on a different skill for achieving more satisfying and authentic outcomes:

- Differentiating between fault and responsibility

- Setting limits

- Establishing the rules of reciprocity

- Promoting optimal awareness by providing positive feedback

- Integrating your optimal tool: raw truth

Differentiating between Fault and Responsibility

Your husband, Steven, arrives twenty minutes late to pick you up at the train station. Without offering you any greeting, explanation, or apology, he proceeds to yell at you about how he's never going to agree to do this again: "I swear, Sharon, don't even start with me. I had to leave my associates at the country club, where I also left my cell phone, wade through obnoxious traffic, and now deal with the predictable sour expression on your face. Who needs this!"

You smack him in the head with your purse, jump out of the car, and get back on the train, never to see him again. Okay, got that fantasy out of your system? Now let's move on to a more productive strategy.

You maintain a moment of silence, giving Steven a chance to hear the echoes of his ugliness bouncing off the windows of the car while you gather your composure. You remind yourself that this isn't about you. Steven has stepped in his own way again. You glance over at him just long enough to try to catch a glimpse of the lost little boy underneath his mean and scowling veneer. You take an easy breath, engage your empathy, and say, "I understand how important it is for you to protect yourself from embarrassment with your associates, and from the dread of letting me down. True, I was

annoyed—and a bit worried too. I'm sure it was frustr
not having your phone to call me. I understand that y
to be angry with you for being late, because I don't alwa
job of expressing disappointment. I care about all of
even the aggravation of dealing with traffic. But it's difficult for me
to feel any tenderness for you when you're so critical and hostile
toward me. I'd like to feel connected, but to do that I need you to
communicate with more consideration for my feelings as well as
your own. On that note, once you've had a chance to calm down,
I'd appreciate an apology."

The momentary silence appears to be seeding some thoughts.
Do you perhaps detect a sobered look on his face? But it's gone in a
flash and he says, "Oh please, don't hit me with that psychobabble
stuff about my feelings again. I'm angry because I knew this would
happen, and I also knew that you'd be pissed off if I didn't agree to
pick you up. That's all. Don't go making it my fault. I had a lot on
my plate today too."

Maybe you're back to that fantasy, where you smack him upside
the head. I know; this is hard work. Nevertheless, you patiently
assign responsibility to him once again, without faulting him:
"Look, Steven, I appreciate that you agreed to help me out today.
I'm not blaming you for the things that were outside of your control
in trying to get here on time. It isn't your fault that you feel upset.
However, it is your responsibility to figure out how to express those
feelings without blaming me or putting me down. Doing otherwise
is simply unacceptable. This behavior is hurtful to me and to our
marriage."

He is quiet again, then nods slowly. A break in the storm? He
drives on and mutters a soft "Yeah, okay." Well… it's a beginning.

In this scene, you are poised within the schema-proof shelter of
your steady and wisely discerning mind. You have mastered the
trigger that formerly would have made you sit and stew, feeling
helpless and angry. You sense certain schema-driven reflexes in
your fantasy response, but your newly acquired understanding of
Steven's issues, the love you still carry for him, and your

compassionate advocacy for yourself have enabled you to generate a new script for this interaction. You emphasize responsibility over fault, and you call attention to the validity of your own needs. You also offer understanding and generosity to the shamed little boy who wants to be liked and appreciated. After all, you've chosen to work on saving your marriage at this point in time.

Again, this is very hard work. Though you can probably identify with scenarios like this one, you may be inclined to predict a less favorable outcome. You may not feel completely satisfied with the way this one concluded. And while it may not be good enough yet, it's a start. Keep in mind that habits are tough to change—both for you and for the narcissist. The brain is a malleable organ, but it usually takes time, repetition, and persistent effort to create enduring changes. For change to occur, you need to look at how long you've been driving in the same gear, unable to mount the steep incline. Sometimes you have to switch gears. New scripts and new ways of communicating may feel contrived at first, but they can become your memorized, signature lyrics over time if they reflect your wise and affirmed voice. The power of being present in your calm and centered mind can make you feel like "waking up alive," as one client put it, meaning he could feel himself experiencing what was happening in the moment. With mindfulness, he wasn't deadened by the distorted beliefs from his old, maladaptive tapes.

Setting Limits

When your daughter is just an infant, your boss calls and says he needs you to travel out of town on business. This is the first time you've had to be away from your daughter overnight, and you're wracked with guilt and worry. Because your husband works the night shift and you didn't have enough advance notice to line up a caregiver, you reluctantly agree to let your mother-in-law take care of the baby in your absence. But when you call home to check in, you're confronted with a tyranny of shoulds, musts, and have tos from your mother-in-law. If it wasn't so insulting, it might be humorous that your mother-in-law had actually moved the dresser and nightstand out of the baby's room because they weren't a good feng shui fit.

As painful as the incident is, it motivates you to learn how to set limits with your narcissistic mother-in-law using empathic confrontation. You begin by trying to understand her behavior and its roots in her past experience. Then you hold her accountable for her actions in the here and now. When you return home, you first tell her how much you appreciate her help, especially since she too had to change her schedule at the last minute. Then you address her troublesome behavior: "I also appreciate how important it is for you to maintain certain standards, and I admire what you've done in your home. However, we'd appreciate it if you wouldn't try to impose your standards on our home. I'm also happy that you and the baby are forming a relationship, but please respect our parenting and household decisions, even if you don't agree with them. If you aren't sure about something, feel free ask us. This will help us protect our relationship and not carry any resentments."

You may be thinking, *Are you kidding me? The narcissist in my life would just ignore me, tell me off, or start World War III if I said something like that.* Yet even if she does respond in these ways, you can continue to set limits while also responding with whatever empathy you can muster. If the narcissist ignores you or humors you in a condescending way, you can call her on it, saying something like "I know you aren't used to having people challenge you, and I'm not looking to have a debate. I'm just respectfully letting you know that this subject isn't open to negotiation. I'm sorry if that upsets you. That isn't my intention." If she resorts to anger or aggression, establish that you won't tolerate that kind of treatment. Maintaining your calm, simply say, "This conversation can't continue if you speak to me that way." If she persists, hang up or walk away. At least you'll know that you tried to improve the relationship by both advocating for yourself and extending empathy to the narcissist. Of course, if the narcissist in question is one of your in-laws, you'll also need the cooperation of your partner. The two of you will need to present a united front in any attempts to set limits.

Establishing the Rules of Reciprocity

It's Saturday night and your boyfriend, Chris, has just announced that the two of you will be dining at his favorite restaurant—again. You have, for the most part, been a good sport about this predictable event. You know how critical he can be about the quality of food and service and how much he enjoys being treated like a celebrity when he walks into this particular establishment, where he's always warmly greeted by the manager and seated right away. You, on the other hand, often drop your head in shame as you walk past those who are waiting as they eyeball you with annoyance. But you were thinking it might be fun to try a new place tonight.

When you suggest the idea, Chris is already frowning after your first few words and cuts you off, saying, "I'm not going to be a guinea pig for some brand-new place, where we'll probably have to wait to be seated and who knows what the food is really like. Forget it." He brushes by you and announces the time that you should be ready to leave for dinner "as planned."

You watch him as he disappears into his newspaper. You steal a second or two so that you might see the picture of Chris as a child emerge before you, the one you keep tucked in your wallet, right next to yours. You thoughtfully imagine the little guy in Chris who was never shown how to share, how to play fair, how to give and take—the boy who was emasculated by his dad and smothered by his mom. Little Chris was very confused and uncomfortable when it came to relationships and fitting in. Taking another brief moment, you reflect on the image of yourself as a child. She was always afraid of getting yelled at for one thing or another. She did her best to try to please everyone to avoid disappointing them or feeling guilty. She didn't know what else to do.

You smile inwardly at little Chris and little you, take a deep, calming breath, and say, "Chris, I think we need to talk about what just happened. I know how much you enjoy dining at the Royal Café. I understand how much it means to you to be treated nicely and to have your favorite meal prepared just the way you like it. With the exception of feeling a bit bad about the people who have to wait in line while we're seated, I've had some nice times there with you. You could have explained your feelings to me when I proposed a change. I don't appreciate being cut off and dismissed. I'm simply requesting that we try something different. I agree with you that the new place may not be a great last-minute choice. But couldn't we be a little adventurous? Perhaps we could come up with a different plan that works for both of us. What do you think?"

Chris, who has made no eye contact with you up until now, peers over his newspaper and somewhat cynically says, "If you know how much I like our usual plan, why do I need a new adventure?" He returns to his reading.

Without missing a beat, you reply, "Chris, I'd really appreciate it if you'd look at me when you're talking to me, as I do with you. I'd like to receive the same courtesy that you expect from me." Chris looks up and you continue: "Thank you. I'm happy to consider your wishes, and I'd like the same from you. This is a two-way street. I'm merely proposing compromise—some give-and-take when it comes to how we spend our time together. If this relationship is going to work, we both need to feel like we matter, like our feelings, opinions, and desires are heard and considered. It sometimes feels like there are different rules for each of us, and that isn't acceptable."

With an unexasperated tone, Chris says, "Okay, I get it. We can talk about it. But please, just not this weekend. I promise we can try something new next time. I just don't feel prepared to do it tonight." You thank him for hearing you, and whether he's really gotten it yet or not, you are determined to hold him to his promise.

There is no actual apology in this scene. Chris offers a simple acknowledgment and makes a promise. You aren't sure he really got it. But he does abort his cynicism and is able to respond in a kinder tone, with eye contact. The emphasis here is on your proposal for fairness, reciprocity, and taking turns. As you fast-forward from this scene, the yardstick for measuring progress is whether he keeps his word without begrudging you. You may have to follow up and reiterate the importance of getting your needs met in the relationship. You may have to express disappointment if he fails to remember and returns to his automatic self-centered policies.

Promoting Optimal Awareness by Providing Positive Feedback

While preparing for the annual holiday dinner at your house, you answer a phone call from your narcissistic brother, Rick. He's calling to wish you a good holiday, and to tell you that he'll be a little late due to some unexpected problems. He usually shows a complete lack of courtesy when running late by not calling at all or calling but saying something like "Listen, I'm running late. I don't know why you have to plan dinner so early. You're just too uptight and ridiculous, Susan." Click. However, this time he says, "Hi, Susan. I know this might seem like my typical pattern, and I'm sorry to hold up dinner for everyone, but due to some unforeseen problems here at home, I'll be about twenty minutes late. Is there anything I can bring?"

You immediately think, *Wrong number?* But then you gather yourself and say, "Gee, thanks, Rick. I hope everything is okay. I appreciate your thoughtfulness in calling, and I'd love for you to bring along a couple of extra serving spoons, please. Thanks for asking." You have a quick realization that this is truly a first in your relationship with your brother. You've spent many years seeding this relationship with honest communication and nourishing it with empathic confrontation, and you're finally seeing the fruits of your labor. You go on to say, "You know, Rick, I'm really grateful for the efforts you're making to be more considerate of me. It really makes me feel closer to you. Thanks again."

He says, "Yeah, I am trying. This would have been a real problem for us in the past. Thanks for noticing."

Offering positive feedback when appropriate is as important as confronting bad behavior in your relationship with the narcissist (and with anyone, for that matter). Yes, Rick is late again. He may still have issues of time management that need to be addressed. But he's making a noticeable effort to be responsible and thoughtful in his actions. You've been tilling this soil with him for a long time, utilizing your complete set of tools. Pointing out the positive—his thoughtful efforts and simple acts of kindness—is exactly what you need to do to escort him toward a feeling of being lovable in an ordinary human way.

In this scene, you didn't overstate your appreciation or use words like "wonderful," "great," "perfect," and so on. You didn't refer to his extraordinary job, car, or vocabulary, as you might have in the past, in order to get his attention or keep him in a good mood. You just offered a simple recognition and a thank-you for being conscious and fairly considerate. Remember, in order for the narcissist to feel comfortable and connected in relationships, he must learn what he never learned as a child: that he is fine for who he is underneath the bulky layers of glitz and gloss. When tenderness, love, and acceptance replace fleeting adulation, he won't feel he needs to prove anything. He won't need to maintain top billing on the shiny grand marquee.

Integrating Your Optimal Tools: Compassion and Raw Truth

It's Thursday, and you arrive home from another jam-packed day of presentations and staff meetings. This has been one of your most challenging weeks at work ever. After greeting your husband, Ed, with a hug, you say that you'd really appreciate having some time to work out and work off some of the day's stress before dinner. He says, "Sure, whatever." But as he says this, you notice his face begins to contort, suggesting a rising irritation. Before you can inquire, he says, "You know, Karen, I'm sick of your selfishness, and I'm also sick of that stupid job of yours. Why don't you just quit and find something else to do with yourself. I have had it with the late dinners and your obsession with your workouts. I don't need this crap anymore. I have more important things to do with my time than sit around waiting for you. There are people who would give anything to be with me. What do I look like, an idiot?" He stares intensely at you.

You're stunned and think, *Here he goes again.* You feel the familiar sensation of heat surging through your chest, splotching your neck, reddening your face. You may feel like screaming out in defense, running to another room to cry, or apologizing and telling Ed he's right. Remember: fight, flight, or freeze. But instead, you pause, breathe, and take a reading on your emotions to see if you can give them a steady and earnest voice without succumbing to those three typical responses to threat. If you're too upset to be empathically confrontational, take some time out to calm yourself and connect with the present moment before returning to the scene. (I'll discuss time-outs later in this chapter.) Finding yourself sufficiently self-possessed, you look Ed in the eye, fully aware of the little boy within who struggled with feelings of loneliness and unworthiness. You summon up your recollections of the little girl in you who had such a difficult time asserting herself and trusting her own feelings.

Then, in a calm voice, bolstered by self-advocacy, you say, "You know, Ed, I don't believe a word of that. It's not that I think you're lying. It's just that I know you, and I know how difficult it can be for you to tell me that you miss me. When I'm distracted, like this week, you often feel as if you're unimportant to me. I can understand how upsetting that must be for you. But there's no need to put me down or blame my job. You aren't giving me a chance to care about you when you speak to me that way. When you get angry and start threatening me, that only causes me to feel hurt and also angry. Your feelings mean a lot to me. But you destroy the chance for us to work things out when you don't acknowledge your own feelings. I'd like to start this conversation over. How about you?"

Ed looks at you in disbelief. You didn't run away, fight back, or give in. This disarms him momentarily. Then, as his mistrust and discomfort settle back in, he says, "Don't tell me how I feel. I already told you. And, by the way, I am angry. That's right—angry."

You can see the little boy within Ed, stomping his foot, crossing his arms, and secretly wishing that his mom or dad would come and hold him and take the pain away. You sense how he's holding on to his protective armor. The timbre of his voice has changed. Although his words underscore his anger, he seems to be more engaged with you, as if prompting you to reinforce the message. You move toward him and reply, "Listen, Ed, I get that you feel angry. But the way you express it only pushes me away. I don't think you really want to push me away. I think you want me to hear you and to love you. I'm only asking that you look behind the anger and tell me about the hurt I can sense as I stand here next to you." You reach to take his hand.

He sheepishly allows you to take his hand and says in a slightly whiny but gentler tone, "Listen, Karen, I know it's been a tough week for you. But it's tough for me too. That's all. Sorry. Go do your workout. I'll be fine."

You're so pleased by this shift. You've reached him. You've extracted the little boy from underneath the mask of the angry fire-breathing dragon. You have wrapped your brain around his vulnerability, as well as your own. It takes tremendous courage to stand up to a dragon with only a single weapon, and an untraditional one at that: compassion. You thank Ed for listening and acknowledge his feelings. You offer to do a shorter workout and propose that the two of you spend some extra time together tonight. He accepts your offer.

You may be thinking that this is just another form of enabling bad behavior by not punishing Ed in some way or ensuring that he has to deal with the consequences. You may feel like you could never say something like that and really mean it when the narcissist is being so insensitive to you. And you may have thoughts like *Who needs to put up with that. Just leave him.* In fact, any or all of these perspectives may be accurate. Sometimes a relationship with a narcissist is so eroded that the best thing you can do for yourself is to set limits or exit the relationship. It may be that you've served out generous portions of empathic confrontation and even compassion but haven't seen any results. Or you may be so wounded that you simply don't have the strength or desire to engage in this process. If so, that's okay. There's no single right or wrong decision; there are only finite choices with consequences. But if you're reading this book, chances are you've chosen to stay connected with the narcissist in your life. Once you develop the capacity to integrate mindful awareness with self-advocacy for your own reasonable rights and needs, you'll find that the empathic confrontation approach often leads to more satisfying results.

Creating Leverage for Change

Earlier in the book, I mentioned that it's very difficult to achieve change in your relationship with a narcissist in the absence of leverage. In the preceding scenes, the implication that the relationship could collapse created leverage. These are relationships of importance: spouse or romantic partner, in-laws, and siblings. In these relationships, both parties have chosen to stay connected to each other. Leverage is built in when the relationship matters and the narcissist doesn't want to lose you. Therefore, it isn't advantageous to create leverage by carelessly or cruelly threatening the narcissist. This would only create ugliness. Instead, create leverage by emphasizing how much the relationship means to you and conveying your fear that it will fall apart if the two of you don't collaborate on making it better. Let's take a look at three important tools for enhancing leverage in your relationship: the implicit assumption rule, the micro to macro approach, and time-outs.

The Implicit Assumption Rule

The implicit assumption rule is more familiarly known as giving someone the benefit of the doubt. You suggest to the narcissist that he probably doesn't appreciate how hurtful his words are and that you assume that he didn't mean to be so critical, but that it did upset you. Remember, most narcissists don't really intend to harm; rather, they seek to protect themselves. Nonetheless, it does hurt and they must be held accountable. You can maintain leverage and avoid destructive and defensive arguments if you preface your statements by conveying your trust in the narcissist's goodwill.

The Micro to Macro Approach

The micro to macro approach is more commonly known as a dress rehearsal. Despite the narcissist's protestations that he doesn't really give a hoot what people think of him, you know that being liked and accepted by others is desirable to all of us, including, and especially, the narcissist. Your private eyewitness observations of his unfavorable behavior represent a microcosm of his relationships with others and the world at large.

In this approach, you empathically point out that his entitled and self-aggrandizing behavior is understandable to you because you're aware of the confusing messages he received as a child: perhaps one moment he was spoiled, and the next he was deprived and ignored. You tell him you know he seeks to gain status by ignoring the rules and expecting special attention from others. Then you explain that, while you've worked hard to understand his makeup and care enough to be open with him and even forgiving, those who don't know him in this way may see him as arrogant, have little desire to be with him, and may not care enough to tell him the truth. This enhances your leverage because he can't hide from your compassion and soothing wisdom, and he also can't deal with the pain of perpetual exclusion.

Time-Outs

In order to maintain leverage with the narcissist, you need to be heard. If you're in a heightened state of anger and at the threshold of a toxic verbal discharge or withdrawal, you may need time to de-escalate your feelings and deconstruct the precipitating events that pushed your hot buttons. Doing so will help you maximize your potential for being heard. Self-help books for couples and on anger management are chock-full of suggestions to take a time-out when flooded with overwhelming feelings or an escalation of anger. This is good advice. Time-outs can be very helpful for de-escalation and self-reflection and also allow the physiological effects of the fight, flight, or freeze response to subside.

John Gottman, an internationally known expert in relationships and how to predict divorce, discusses the challenges and importance of calming down before engaging in healing communication after a rupturing episode (Gottman and Silver 2004). He points out that while many well-adjusted and reportedly happy couples can fight without harmful consequences to their relationship, couples who have a fragile connection to one another fight in damaging ways and often need time to stabilize their turbulent emotional and physiological states before entering the repair zone.

The time-out is often defined as each person seeking out some temporary distance from the other, perhaps by going to another room of the house or taking a walk for some negotiated amount of time. The idea is to have a cooling-off period before revisiting the disputed issue or even just being around each other. In schema therapy, we also recommend that when you're triggered and your body and mind become flooded with overwhelming or angry sensations, it's best to seek out a temporary refuge to catch your breath and regain your emotional equilibrium. But what can you do during a time-out to help you to get comfortable in your own skin again?

Breathe

Those gentle, calming breaths you use in your mindfulness practice (described in chapter 5) can be helpful. During a time-out, settle in and dedicate a few moments to feeling the rise and fall of your abdomen, your lungs expanding and contracting, the coolness of the air you inhale, and the warmth of your exhalation. With each breath, bathe your mind and body in lulling tranquility and vibrant clarity.

Use a Schema Flash Card

Keep a flash card or two that can act as a prompt for identifying the schema you've fallen prey to and awakening you to the here and now. The flash card can act as a guide in directing you toward healthier responses. One the flash card, utilize the four steps you learned in chapter 4 (observe, assess, identify, and differentiate) and add a final step of looking for healthy ways to soothe yourself:

1. **Observe:** Notice the feelings you're experiencing.

2. **Assess:** Link the corresponding schemas to these feelings, as well as to your reactions.

3. **Identify:** Label the feelings and responses that may be schema driven.

4. **Differentiate:** Let go of the phantoms of the past and notice yourself from a here-and-now perspective.

5. **Self-soothe:** Look for healthy ways to soothe yourself in the present moment.

Here's how that might look:

1. *I'm aware that I'm feeling furious with the narcissist.*

2. *My emotional deprivation and self-sacrifice schemas are getting activated because I feel misunderstood and resent being taken for granted.*

3. *I want to scream and punish him. I also notice food cravings.*

4. *These are the feelings of the powerless little girl who had to make tremendous sacrifices to feel appreciated and noticed. But I don't need to prove anything now. I have choices. I'm not powerless, and I do have rights in this relationship. Spewing anger at the narcissist is useless. Bingeing on unhealthy foods may be soothing momentarily, but it can only camouflage my pain, not heal it. I have a right to feel angry, but I don't need to become the anger. I am a capable adult who understands the narcissist's issues and quirks and my own. I can be an effective spokesperson for my feelings and a good advocate for my vulnerable self. I must advocate for myself without acting out.*

5. *Instead of flipping into angry mode or suppressing my feelings with food, I could do something else:*

   - *Write in my journal for five minutes.*

   - *Call my friend who always knows how to calm and reassure me when I feel like this.*

   - *Write down and practice what I'd like to communicate and how I'll say it when we take the issue up again.*

Engage in Distraction

Healthy distractions can also be valuable for stabilizing your mood and calming your emotions while in time-out mode. Here are some suggestions:

- Read or write poetry.

- Listen to music.

- Do a crossword puzzle.

- Organize.

- Make a to-do list.

- Dance or sing.

- Exercise.

- Meditate.

- Take a bath.

- Get a massage.

The Role of Empathy in the Therapeutic Relationship

Many partners and family members of narcissists ask me, "What happens in therapy with a narcissist or with a couple with these issues? How do I find the right therapist? What should I be looking for in a therapist, and what's the most effective approach for treating narcissism?"

The therapist shouldn't simply be a nice listener who reflectively validates the narcissist's complaints and rigid avoidance. The therapist must also be firm and able to withstand the narcissist's anger or criticism. If the therapist is too passive, the narcissist will probably waste a lot of time showing off, blaming, seeking approval, and possibly taunting the therapist. If the therapist is intimidated, the narcissist will sense it, seek to dominate the therapist, and hijack therapy or end it. And while the therapist must be knowledgeable about narcissism, she must be more than an expert in theory; she must be authentic. If the therapist is too intellectual, there's a risk that this will reinforce the narcissist's competitive and detached coping modes.

The therapist must also have an authentic curiosity and utilize empathy, understanding and being capable of emotional resonance with these difficult clients. This means making an effort to experience the internal world of the client, though not necessarily agreeing with the client or extending compassion or sympathy. Indeed, empathic confrontation is one of the most important skills in treating these clients. I often use this approach with narcissistic clients, saying things like, "Yes, I get that your dad gave you the message that you were entitled to special privileges. But the world doesn't work that way, and he didn't prepare you to live in this world, especially when it comes to taking responsibility for the impact of your reactions on others and allowing yourself to be truly loved. And I have to tell you that the way you're speaking to me right now is very off-putting and distracting. I imagine it must be hard for people to hear you when they're distracted by this offensive tone."

In therapy, empathic awareness is the launching pad for setting limits and holding clients accountable for unkind acts and lack of remorse. Sometimes it opens the door to deeper investigations. Persistently pushing against the narcissist's defiant avoidance and emotional detachment can help alter self-defeating patterns and intolerable emotions that have kept him stuck.

Finally, the therapist must be authentic, tell the truth, and be mindful, operating in and reflecting moment-to-moment experiences in the therapy relationship. Narcissists have a lot of mistrust, especially of people who care about them. Illuminating the truth through a process of discovery creates a bond that allows for safety and trust in the therapeutic relationship. Ultimately, the therapist must be capable of telling the truth to a narcissistic client and setting limits without disparaging the client. In this way, the therapist helps reparent the client, enhancing his healthy adult self by meeting the core needs of the vulnerable part buried within.

Conclusion

Change can be an arduous and exasperating undertaking. Not everyone is ready or willing to change or even interested in doing so. Fear can be a primary obstacle, including fear of awakening the dreadful feelings embedded in schemas, even if the goal is to assuage those feelings. But given all that you've learned about the brain, you know that change is possible. You may feel a restored sense of hope. In this chapter, you've had a chance to see that possibility in action. You've sampled some of the most crucial implements for inspiring change: empathic confrontation, compassion, self-advocacy, setting limits, and maintaining leverage.

In the final chapter of the book, I'll continue to guide you through strategies that will further accessorize your new linguistic ensemble. Previous points will be reiterated, elaborated, and tailored to fit your needs.

chapter 8

Making the Most of a Difficult Situation: Seven Gifts of Communication with a Narcissist

The artist is nothing without the gift, but the gift is nothing without work.

—Émile Zola

Each of us has a personal communication style that results from a combination of temperament and adopted and practiced skills, funneled through spoken and written words, gestures, facial expressions, behaviors, and body language as a means of relating to and connecting with others. The gifts of communication discussed in this chapter are nothing like the "gift of gab," which refers to the ability to go on and on and on about anything. Rather, they are the benefits you can reap, both personally and interpersonally, from authentic communication appropriate to the context and undertaken with integrity. They are also the gifts you offer to others when you communicate thoughtfully and carefully, with attention to not just what you're saying but how you're saying it.

Just as the word "gift" has several different meanings, the gifts of communication with a narcissist exist on various levels. A gift can be either something voluntarily given to another or the very act of giving. "Gift" can also refer to natural qualities or capabilities, and when used in this sense, it usually implies inborn talents. In terms of communication, this would suggest that a person has an innate forte for touching the hearts and souls of others. However, a talent can also be developed through practice and intention. I view gifted communicators as people who have actively cultivated a facility for listening to their inner wisdom and making sense out of their lives, just as you've been doing throughout this book. Gifted communicators know the value of observing, listening, and probing the world beyond their own skin. They express themselves and engage in dialogue with elegance, grace, and thoughtfulness. The good news is that we can all develop this talent.

By now, you've learned a great deal about yourself, particularly in regard to your relationship with the narcissist in your life. You've acquired a new degree of inner wisdom and have learned and honed skills for embracing the present moment and distinguishing between truth and fiction. You have a new awareness and perhaps a more empathically attuned heart and mind, enabling you to peel back the layers of the narcissist to find the vulnerable, lonely soul at his core. You can stand up for yourself without being defensive because you feel no need to defend. You can make a thoughtful request without resorting to a counterattack. You can anticipate the likelihood of imperfect and even unsettling moments and accept this possibility with less angst because you have a new set of skills for repairing and mending these interactions. You're unburdened by the newfound realization that none of us have the authority or even the ability to change someone else. However, you've developed skills in self-expression and attuned listening that serve to create a positive impact, wedging open a new space where change can occur. You have the potential to package and share your gifts through your own personally crafted art of communication.

Harnessing the Force

You might be familiar with the phrase "May the Force be with you," from Star Wars. The philosophy of the Jedi knights suggests that a sentient, interplanetary energy lies within us all, binding us together and giving us the power to withstand opposition and create light in moments of darkness. I'd like to suggest a similar approach, captured by the acronym FORCE, which stands for flexibility, openness, receptivity, competence, and enlightenment.

When your mind is actively engaged in this state of FORCE, your interactions will be more authentic and rewarding and you can share your wisdom in a way that sheds a warm and brilliant light on darker moments. When interacting with difficult people, make use of your heightened empathy and sharpened focus to manifest all of the elements of the FORCE:

- **Flexibility:** Adjust your statements, questions, and responses to fit the situation. Resist and discard rigid and unbendable inclinations and ideas.

- **Openness:** Listen without judgment or preconceived expectations. By not jumping to conclusions, you allow discovery to occur.

- **Receptivity:** Use eye contact, facial expression, and body language, combined with your words and tone of voice, to suggest that you are ready to relate to others and invite their ideas and feelings without coercion, interruption, or censorship.

- **Competence:** Be a credible and empathic listener and display clarity and sensibility when communicating, along with enthusiastic and attuned listening. Be a role model of authenticity, and don't be motivated by obtaining recognition.

- **Enlightenment:** Be curious. Encourage and demonstrate interest in exchanging insights. Create an atmosphere of mutual awareness and understanding through spoken and unspoken language, shining the light of knowledge on the darkness of ignorance and inviting others to do the same for you.

Being self-possessed permits you to tap into your personal FORCE. But here's the irony: The art of effective communication, which contains all the elements of the FORCE, cannot be effective if it's *forced*. It must emerge as naturally and gracefully as leaves unfold in spring. Though your inner resources may seem difficult to access, they do lie within. If you have suffered the slings and arrows of a self-sacrifice or subjugation schema, it's important to realize that becoming self-possessed doesn't mean becoming selfish. It simply means equalizing the ratio of giving and receiving—getting off the tiresome one-way street that inevitably leads to the narcissist. Being self-possessed means being informed by an illuminated consciousness and steady confidence. It means becoming personally defined. Everything you've learned from this book, and from other sources of information and support you've explored, will guide the way.

If your new skills enable you to create a rewarding and reciprocal relationship with the narcissist, you'll undoubtedly feel an enormous burden has been lifted. A satisfying relationship is undoubtedly among the greatest gifts life has to offer. In addition, your mastery of effective communication with the narcissist can generalize into effective communication in other challenging interactions. After all, if you can successfully handle one of the biggest button pushers on the planet, you can handle almost anyone.

Presenting Your Gifts

Throughout this book, you've collected many tools for surviving and thriving in a relationship with a narcissist. It won't be an easy journey, but with time you'll learn to wield these tools more adeptly and in concert. Your tools—identifying schemas, anticipating difficult encounters, being mindful, engaging in self-reflection, directing a calming focus on the breath, using empathic confrontation, extending compassion, and all the others—are designed to integrate with each other to ignite your inner FORCE, invigorate your voice, and strengthen your stance as you enter into difficult interpersonal encounters.

It's similar to what's involved in playing tennis: You need to anticipate the other person's actions, move to be in position to respond, keep your eye on the ball, adjust your response as needed, make strong and consistent contact with the ball, and follow through—and then be ready to do it all again. It takes practice to integrate all of these moves and skills into the well-choreographed synchronous flow that produces a satisfying shot.

Up to this point, I've focused on communication skills specific to the challenges of dealing with a narcissist. Here are a few other, more general communication skills you can use to help heighten the effectiveness of the skills you've been working on:

- **Matching impact to intention:** Craft what you say and how you say it so that it's received by the listener as you intended. Keep in mind what you hope to communicate and choose words and ways of expressing yourself that will ensure the other person receives the message you'd like to impart. For example, if you're aware that you're very angry but would primarily like to communicate that you feel lonely, you'll need to consciously express yourself in a way that communicates loneliness rather than anger.

- **Modeling:** Give the other person an example of what you expect in return. For example, if you speak calmly and respectfully, you'll have a better chance of getting the same in response.

- **Having reasonable expectations:** Know your listener and what he is capable of, and know yourself and what you feel capable of in that moment. Some days are better than others for engaging in the challenge of communicating about difficult matters. Listen to your mind and body, and choose your battles thoughtfully.

In addition to all of the skills and insights you've collected for surviving and thriving in your relationship with a narcissist, the seven gifts of communication detailed below will complement your craft and enrich all of your relationships—not just the difficult ones! Each gift is illustrated with a vignette, and although most of these vignettes describe interactions between couples, they are equally relevant to relationships with people other than a romantic partner: parent, friend, sibling, boss, neighbor—you name it. Also, keep in mind that in order for this artful employment of communication to be effective, you must come prepared with steady eye contact; a gently paced, confident, and clear voice; a patient ear; and, of course, the FORCE, a flexible, open, receptive, competent, and enlightened state of mind.

The Seven Gifts

By communicating with integrity and self-disclosure, you offer valuable gifts to those you interact with. Sharing yourself and your inner strength and wisdom in this way will also help you bolster your sense of self-worth—and help the narcissist in your life do the same, healing the insecure and damaged child within. This further opens the door to the possibility of positive change in your relationship. Each gift is associated with a specific form of artful communication. As you model these seven arts, the narcissist in your life can, potentially, become a more effective communicator, closing the circle and allowing you to become the beneficiary of these same gifts. Of course, there are countless arts of communication, each with a complement of gifts embedded within, but for our purposes, the following seven are the most relevant:

1. The art of mutual respect is an expression of the gift of generosity.

2. The art of self-disclosure is an expression of the gift of courage.

3. The art of discernment is an expression of the gift of truth.

4. The art of collaboration is an expression of the gift of shared effort.

5. The art of anticipating clashes is an expression of the gift of foresight.

6. The art of apology is an expression of the gift of responsibility.

7. The art of reflective listening is an expression of the gift of balance.

1. The Art of Mutual Respect

Mutual respect entails acknowledging differences between yourself and others without negative labeling. This is the gift of generosity. You accept the narcissist's different point of view or preference without becoming critical, defending your position, or discarding your own opinions. You know that, while there is hardly a challenge when the two of you see things eye to eye, differences can set the stage for a long, drawn-out drama. You're aware that understanding something doesn't necessarily mean agreeing with it. You're committed to understanding, compromise, and mutual respect for one another's thoughts, beliefs, and desires. You expect the same in return.

Let's say that your husband tells you, "I've decided on whom I plan to hire to take care of the lawn and garden this season," and you have another position on the subject. You reply in a way that communicates mutual respect: "I can understand how strongly you feel about hiring Mr. Landscaper, and I'd like to be considerate of your desire to do so. I appreciate the effort you always put into researching the options. I know the beauty and upkeep of the property is important to you. I'm open to your plan, but I'd like to discuss it further. I'm feeling a bit conflicted about our options because my friend Jude's son is so desperately in need of work right now, and I'd feel bad about not giving him the job. I know it's risky mixing friendship with business, but I'd like to give him a chance. I hear that he's very good. Can we think it through together? Perhaps you can help me to see why this may or may not be the best option." Should the narcissist respond in an entitled, impatient, or condescending manner, you can reach back into chapter 7 to use the implicit assumption rule (giving the other person the benefit of the doubt) and establish reciprocity.

2. The Art of Self-Disclosure

Self-disclosure allows you to unburden yourself of withholding the truth. This is the gift of courage. Securely attached to your inner strength, you discard your habitual murmur and reveal your fuller, more vibrant experience to the narcissist—without the use of gratuitous insult. Even though it often seems counterintuitive to expose your vulnerability to him, like trying to hug a snarling dog, you've learned that his bark is a protective device; perhaps he's more like a sheep in wolf's clothing. You don't divulge yourself in order to make him feel like he's a terrible person, but instead to help him appreciate the impact of his behavior on you. When you are no longer willing to toil in the salt mines of passive nods, acceptance of character assaults, and hopeless resignation, this gift will liberate the possibility for real communication.

Let's say that your husband comes home from work and, in a scowling, growling tone, says, "You know, I am sick and tired of walking into this house and finding you on the phone. Look at this place. Where's today's mail? Would it kill you to be free to talk to me for a change? Oh, forget it."

You take a calming breath, then reply: "I know it makes you feel bad, as if you don't matter to me, when you get home and find me on the phone. I understand, and I'm sorry that it makes you feel that way. I look forward to seeing you, but I need some help in predicting when you'll get home, since it varies each day. I also need you to know that when you speak to me this way, it hurts. I know that you don't intend the words to hurt me, but they do. And when I feel hurt, it's difficult for me to feel and express loving feelings for you, even though I truly want that in our relationship. I typically just give in or pull away. I don't want to do that anymore. I'd like to work on this together and hope you'd like to as well."

3. The Art of Discernment

When dealing with schemas, which lie at the heart of narcissism and dealing with a narcissist, discernment involves distinguishing between the here and now versus the "there and then." This is the gift of truth. When you offer discernment, you communicate with a clarity that's based in the present moment. You clear the cobwebbed obstacles of the past and enter into the domain of now. You acknowledge history without succumbing to it. Like most of us, the narcissist in your life is prone to letting the automatic nature of memory guide his truth. You can help him distinguish reality in the here and now from automatic beliefs and habits. Because you recognize the importance of paying attention and have been working on this skill, you are adroitly prepared in your role as the wake-up caller.

Let's say that you've asked your husband what time he'd like to leave to go to his father's for dinner and he says, "How many times have we been there now, about a hundred? You know damn well how long it takes to get there. Why are you bothering me with these ridiculous questions? I'm trying to finish this presentation that I'm working on for a very important meeting on Monday. You just don't seem to get how important this is to me, do you? I'd like to keep a roof over our heads, you know, so I have to do well on this project. There's a lot of pressure on me."

You keep a steady grip on the image of a little boy who was always trying to please his dad, only to be consistently met with his father's impatient glare, harsh criticisms, or stone-cold silence, and realize that your husband's response has nothing to do with you or the question you asked. There's a certain incongruousness to his spouting. Though you're offended by his unkindness, you understand the power of his presiding schemas. You keep yourself securely attached to the present and the truth. You look down the long corridor of your own historic emotional residence and see the little girl who would take the blame for anything and everything if it meant keeping the peace at home. Your connection to that old reality has forged sensations in the present that pulse through your mind like an express train headed down a mountain, but you recognize these are old, schema-driven responses.

So you take a deep breath, calm yourself, and look at your husband, tightly bound by the many fears he harbors. Then you say, "I know that you're busy, but I need a few moments of your time. This relationship is important to me. You're right: we've made the trip many times and I know exactly how long it takes to get to your father's house. I understand the pressure you're feeling at work and the burden to maintain our lifestyle. You work very hard, and I appreciate everything you do. I guess I could have been more precise with my question, saying something like 'Do you want to leave early to spend some time with your father before dinner?' I guess you could have just answered the question. Look, honey, it's me—the one who knows you and thinks you're doing a great job, the one who really gets you. This is me—I'm not your dad. I imagine these encounters with your father can bring up all kinds of uncomfortable memories for you, even if you aren't aware of them. It must have been very difficult dealing with him all those years. I know that you're trying to be closer to him now that he's marginally mellowed. Let's not let it spoil things between us. I'm available to listen if you'd like to talk."

If the situation remains heated, consider taking a time-out so both of you can cool down and engage in some self-reflection before reconvening.

4. The Art of Collaboration

Collaboration suggests a collective and invokes the power of "we." This is the gift of shared effort. Though we are all capable of making mistakes, we also have something to offer one another in working together. In a "we" state of communication, your dialogue is carefully sculpted from the philosophic clay of shared responsibility. You're informed by the narcissist's extreme sensitivity to feeling defective and ashamed, his fear of being controlled and taken advantage of, and his inability to ask for connection. You know that he can launch into a mode of entitlement, grandiosity, bullying, or avoidance when his schemas trigger those feelings. Because being collaborative keeps finger-pointing impulses at bay, it helps keep the narcissist at ease.

Cognitive therapists and schema therapists use "we" language with clients to mediate hierarchical struggles in therapy. This means we offer clients our expertise and human experience in identifying feelings and links between historical and current problems. We help them develop strategies in a way that invites them to understand, challenge, question, and have input. We aren't invested in power struggles. The goal of collaboration is to promote an understanding of the issues and find mutually agreeable strategies for change.

When difficult feelings arise during therapy with narcissistic clients, I often say something like "Wow, isn't the brain amazing? One minute you and I are immersed, with curiosity and compassion, in an important investigation of your history or your current challenges, and the next minute we're having uncomfortable feelings with each other. Hmm… Let's look at this." Invoking the collective in such an acknowledgment of a shift in feelings assigns no blame or shame, freeing the narcissist to investigate the triggering event rather than resorting to self-destructive coping modes.

The collaborative approach is especially important with narcissists who are prone to buttoning up their vulnerability behind impermeable inner walls of self-protection. While you can't always predict what will trigger you and the narcissist in your life, you can artfully offer the gift of the collaborative "we" when trying to communicate about how to improve your relationship with one another.

Let's say you, out of guilt or longing, decide to call your narcissistic mother and invite her to spend the day with you and she replies, "I would love to. But please don't take me to that awful restaurant where we ate last time. It was abominable. I raised you to have much better taste than that. And if you want to go shopping, you'd better plan on an early lunch or a late dinner. You know how difficult it is for you to make decisions and to find things that fit you properly. Frankly, I could be happy spending the day in the city, but you often seem to get very nervous there. Oh well, you can decide, dear. I'm sure it will be lovely."

You've worked hard at this relationship and can mostly accept that your mother has many limitations when it comes to expressing her love and appreciation to you. You have learned how to successfully maintain loving, healthy, and healing relationships with others. Before responding, you remind yourself that you love your mother, though you're not always sure why. You maintain a firm grasp on reasonable expectations, along with a sense of humor. You wrap a loving imaginary arm around the pained heart of little you. You peer into a well-formulated understanding of the origins of your mother's narcissism and sense that she loves you even if she humbles most of the time. With that, you can return to the phone and say, "Mom, look how difficult it is for us to ask for what we need from each other. It doesn't really matter to me how we spend the time. I just want to spend it with you. I suppose we could both be a bit amused and a bit saddened by how uncomfortable we seem to get with each other's choices and styles. We need to find a better way to ask for what we need, instead of getting annoyed and critical with each other. If I were starting this conversation over, I'd tell you that it doesn't matter what we do, but I'd love to spend some time together with you. And if what we do matters to you, which is truly fine, we could come up with a plan that suits us both. It would probably be a lot easier and more honest that way. What do you think? Can we start the conversation over again?"

5. The Art of Anticipating Clashes

Anticipating clashes allows you to preempt the predictable pitfalls in your relationship. This is the gift of foresight. This gift is provided in part by the biological makeup of the brain. You are endowed with the ability to draw upon memory to predict what lies ahead. For example, when you know someone long enough and well enough, you may find yourselves finishing sentences for each other. Or how about your memory of the sharp bend in the road on your route to work? It is memory that informs you to initially slow down and then accelerate into the turn in order to avoid losing control of your car. It is the wisdom of what-if and the memory of how-to that keeps you safe. We have a seemingly infinite number of remembered experiences that allow us to preempt troublesome encounters without even thinking about it. Adding your increased mindfulness skills to this already embedded gift, you have not only the sage wisdom of experience within your grasp, but a robust repertoire of on-the-spot reflexes. In your interactions with the narcissist in your life, you can rebuild the very foundation on which your communications are based.

Let's say you haven't seen your father in months. He's invited you to lunch, but now, at the last minute, he calls to cancel for the third time because of his usual work-related priorities. He says, "I'm afraid that I'm going to have to cancel our lunch date again, sweetie. It's work. I have this client who...blah, blah, blah. I could have refused to meet with him, but...yada yada, and, well, you know your old man (chuckle). Now don't go getting sulky with me. I'll call you soon. Okay, gotta go."

You saw this coming since his first invitation to lunch two months ago. You've experienced this pattern repeatedly over many years. Your father has rarely been good at keeping promises to spend time with you. It seems he's only motivated to see you when you're about to make a decision about a car, a job, a vacation, or some major investment without his magnanimous advice. This type of get-together seems more purposeful to him and makes him feel very important—fatherly, in his mind. And, while you appreciate his input—he is a very bright guy, after all—you'd like to feel that he's interested in other parts of you and your life. You have pretty much given up all of your expectations, but not your longings. You want to keep him in your life, perhaps for your children, perhaps even a little bit for you. But you'd like to do so without resentment.

Unfortunately, dealing with him isn't like the sharp bend in the road on the way to work. You've been unable to figure out a way to steer clear of the convolutions in your relationship with your dad and maintain a grip on a securely intact you—until now. With your newly awakened gift of anticipating clashes combined with some forethought about preemptive measures, you can respond to your dad with a secure voice and without blaming, attacking, or sulking. You are aware (more than he is) that he harbors a profound sense of inadequacy and has an emotionally inhibited style of communicating. You know that he overcompensates for his sense of inadequacy through his work and competitiveness, and you know that he can become defensive when confronted about his carelessness with his loved ones. You also know that he needs time to synthesize information and doesn't respond well in the moment.

With this knowledge and plenty of experience in the land of letdowns and disappointments, you reply, "Dad, before you hang up, I'd like to ask for a few moments of your time. I know that this may hurt your feelings. I know that you're sensitive to my opinion of you and that you care very much about me. I know how important your work is to you and how everyone in the family has benefited from your success. I'm grateful for that. But what I'd really like is to have some time with you, just hanging out together for no special reason. Maybe we could just exchange some stories and have a few laughs. I know that you aren't very fond of 'touchy-feely' talk, as you call it, but I miss you, and I'm disappointed when you cancel our dates. I'd especially appreciate it if you could show me more consideration by giving me a little notice. I had to make special arrangements, which I can't change now, in order to see you. I'm not blaming you, Dad. I'm simply asking you to think about the impact on me. I don't want you to feel guilty, but I do wish you understood how I feel. You don't have to respond right now. I know that you're pressed for time. Thanks for listening."

6. *The Art of the Apology*

A genuine apology places emphasis on compassion for the wounded party, not redemption for the transgressor. This is the gift of responsibility. With this gift, you're committed to responsibility for the impacts of your words, sentiments, and behaviors, especially when they're hurtful. You know that your behavior can serve as a model for how you'd like the narcissist to treat you, and you hope for reciprocity. Therefore, you model an apology that's based in a compassionate understanding of how and why certain messages hurt him in the hopes that he'll learn how to offer an apology that reflects an appreciation of your sensitivities as well. You express authentically remorseful feelings that are free of self-loathing and a self-centered preoccupation with guilt. You are grounded in the experience of the other person, not focused on a mission of personal redemption. It's less about you than it is about your responsibility.

Let's say your boyfriend has a problem with people being late and hates to be kept waiting. He places a lot of importance on being prompt and on time, largely because his socialite mother, who was unreliable and haphazard, occasionally forgot to pick him up after school or from a friend's house, leaving him feeling frightened and embarrassed. He's a bit too unforgiving at times, even when unavoidable circumstances interfere with being on time. Therefore, you try to protect his inner child from experiences that would trigger these haunting feelings of fear and humiliation. You value promptness too and don't like to keep others waiting. But lately you've been distracted, stressed, and prone to running late, even with him. You know that recently you've been careless in managing your time and being available, but you haven't been honest about it. Your boyfriend is clearly upset with you, but he tends to distance himself rather than telling you how he feels.

So you take the first step and say, "I'm sorry for the carelessness I've shown lately when it comes to being on time. I sense that you're upset with me, and I understand. Because I have the privilege of knowing your personal history and the issues with your mom, I know how it hurts you when people don't keep their word—especially me. I know how it made you feel forgotten and even foolish in the eyes of others when your mom wasn't responsible. But you aren't a fool, and I haven't forgotten you. It's my problem, and I'm committed to fixing it. I understand how my actions and excuses just keep hurting you. I'm sorry. I don't want to hurt you. While I can't promise that I'll never let you down in this relationship, I will do my best to be more attentive and thoughtful."

You expect only to be heard. Your intention is for your boyfriend to feel soothingly cared for, cradled in your empathy and compassion. You already know that you aren't a bad person. You don't need to be stroked, and you don't need to punish yourself. You can hold yourself accountable for both the positive and negative contributions you make in your relationships. You expect the same from others when appropriate. This effective approach offers an avenue for healing the fractured moments and is also a model of what you expect from the narcissist when it's his turn to responsibly and compassionately repair a tattered encounter.

7. The Art of Reflective Listening

Reflective listening involves mirroring the communication of the other person and extracting hidden sentiments. This is the gift of balance. You know both how to articulate information and how to put self-interest aside and invite your listener to express himself to you. You are an ardent companion in communication who respectfully and patiently allows others to share themselves with confidence, knowing you'll meet them nonjudgmentally. You listen carefully and reflect, without appraisal, an unbiased replay of what you hear in an effort to clarify and validate. And though you may have a different point of view, you wait your turn to express it.

With an awareness of how threatening honest communication can be for the narcissist, you extract hidden meanings and masked vulnerabilities by gently mirroring what you believe remains unspoken. You know that by listening and reflecting you offer the possibility for mutual discoveries—anything from knowledge about a particular subject to handling controversial matters without getting triggered, or from feelings about each other that have been closeted in anger, apathy, or avoidance to a strength you never knew you had or a realization that the narcissist becomes receptive when he feels heard.

Let's say your husband has been suffering from a bad case of creative block and is dreading an upcoming meeting at work to discuss his team's vision for the coming year. Never particularly tolerant of frustration, he has become overly stressed and distracted. In desperation, he decides to put the pressure on a very unseasoned associate to come up with the data for the report. He arrives home from the dreaded meeting, sits down at the table, and begins to tell you about his terrible day, saying, "What a nightmare! How dare that little nobody-of-an-associate try to make me look incompetent at the division meeting today. He's the incompetent one. His delivery was incomprehensible. My partners, my colleagues, hell, even my subordinates, were utterly speechless when he gave that uninspiring report. He tried to lay it on me. Well, you better believe I let him have it. He's lucky to still have his job. Can you imagine? After all I've done for him, carrying him up the ladder. He would be nowhere without me. I knew I couldn't trust him. And don't you go telling me what I could have or should have done. I'm in no mood for your lectures and I'm sick of your 'I told you so' attitude. I don't want to talk about it."

There's a pause, and then he continues: "Didn't I tell you that I never should have let my partners talk me into bringing him into my division? Wasn't I the one who single-handedly took this marketing team to the top last year? Damn right. Everyone there knows it, too, even if they didn't have the nerve or consideration to say so in the meeting."

You've been listening quietly, eyes fixed upon him even though he only occasionally looks directly at you. You felt the mild sting of his characterization of you: the lecturer, the "I told you so" partner. You place that on a mental shelf for now and remain a present and nondefensive listener. You can clearly see the narcissistic injury, in that your husband was unable to take responsibility for his poor judgment in imposing the project, at the last minute, on his novice associate. You shelve that too and remain a present and nonjudgmental listener.

But now that he's allowed an opening for a reflective, extracting, and supportive response, you reply, "It's clear that you're feeling very upset. I know how hard you've worked and how unappreciated you've been feeling there. I know it was a setback to have felt off your stride creatively last week, especially because you feel like there's no one you can count on to share the burden of significant projects and deadlines. It sounds like it's hard, not receiving any support or backup from the team when you feel unfairly represented by a colleague. I can't imagine how difficult it would be for you to admit that you need collaborative help, especially since you take so much pride in your autonomy. I can actually sense your tension resonating in my own body as you describe the experience. Is there anything I can do to help?"

After more venting, some cooling down, and another opening for you to communicate, you revisit parts of the conversation that were more relevant to your relationship: "I heard you say, in the midst of your upset, that you didn't want me to lecture you, and that you predict I'll give you an 'I told you so' response. I wonder if you truly feel that way or if it was just something you said because of how upset and embarrassed you were by the outcome of the meeting."

He clarifies that those statements were mostly due to being upset, but that sometimes he does feel as though you wag the finger and lecture him. You accept his perception and ask him to point it out to you whenever it feels that way because you don't want him to experience you as uncaring or demeaning. (There's no point in pursuing this point without evidence in the moment. It just becomes a "No I didn't" "Yes you did" conflict.)

The next item is a bit trickier. You reflect back that perhaps his anger with his associate is partly a displaced anger with himself for not living up to his own high standards. You gently point out that he's very demanding of himself and that this might make it hard for him to tolerate imperfection in others. You successfully resist feeding his insatiable cravings for admiration and instead nourish him with your appreciation for his honesty in communication, his enthusiasm for doing well, and his untiring dedication to his goals, granting him permission to drop his guard and rest his head on your shoulder every now and then. By offering him this gift of communication, you also model your expectation for reciprocity. He might pick up the cue and learn how to listen to you too.

Conclusion

This chapter described seven gifts inherent in effective communication with the narcissist in your life and the interpersonal arts with which they're associated. When you use these arts to express yourself with integrity, from a state of mind that's flexible, open, receptive, competent, and enlightened, your own personal FORCE is indeed with you.

Artfully applying the seven gifts of communication will promote interactions that are healthier, more satisfying, and more intimate. And as you craft your speaking and listening with thoughtfully chosen words, tone of voice, pacing, eye contact, facial expression, and body language, you'll be modeling what you'd like in return in those difficult interactions. Having a voice that accurately represents you and your intentions is always positive and to your benefit. Sometimes this has to be enough. There are no guarantees and no sure paths to victory in terms of changing someone else. Narcissists typically aren't the sort of people who voluntarily seek help, coaching, or any kind of assistance with breaking down their impenetrable emotional walls. If anything, they avoid this type of interaction at almost all costs, whether through adamant refusal, mockery, externalizing blame onto someone else, or various forms of distraction and hiding.

That being said, you've learned how you can play a vital role in opening the door to the possibility for change, through leverage if need be or perhaps just by offering kindness and compassion. No matter what the outcome in terms of changes in the narcissist or your interactions with him, you can play a significant role in your own liberation from fear, intimidation, subjugation, self-sacrifice, and even abuse by identifying the life themes and schemas of your early experience, paying attention to triggering events and internal cues, setting limits, and adapting your responses to both the narcissist and your own automatic inner dialogue. Liberating this healthy, wise, and awakened self within you is perhaps the ultimate achievement.

All of the strategies in this book have the potential to be highly effective self-help tools in bringing about more satisfying experiences with a narcissist. However, the self-help journey can be both lonely and arduous. Sometimes the help of a professional therapist can be of tremendous value. Schemas can be very rigid and sometimes impenetrable despite your best efforts. Should you choose to seek professional assistance, I recommend you find someone versed in the foundations of cognitive behavioral therapy and trained in schema therapy. In the Resources section, you'll find contact information for organizations that can help you find a therapist.

Resources

Organizations

The Cognitive Therapy Centers listed below, in New Jersey and New York, offer a full range of services to individuals, couples, families, and groups seeking consultation or psychotherapy services. They also provide referrals, ongoing professional supervision, training in schema therapy, and graduate and postgraduate training in cognitive behavioral therapy. In addition, they host a number of skilled speakers who are available for off-site seminars and workshops.

The Cognitive Therapy Center of New Jersey, located in Springfield, New Jersey. The center's director also provides supervision and training to professionals who are interested in learning about interpersonal neurobiology: disarmingthenarcissist.com; (973) 218-1776; wetb@aol.com.

The Cognitive Therapy Center of New York and the Schema Therapy Institute of New York, located in New York City: http. schematherapy.com; (212) 221-0700.

Dr. Dan Siegel has a website offering information on interpersonal neurobiology, along with helpful links: www.drdansiegel.com.

The Gottman Institute, located in Seattle, Washington, offers workshops for couples and training for professionals: http.gottman. com; (888) 523-9042.

The National Domestic Violence Hotline: http.ndvh.org; (800) 799-7233, (800) 787-3224 (TTY).

Recommended Reading

Beck, A. T. 1991. *Cognitive Therapy and the Emotional Disorders.* London: Penguin Books.

Beck, A. T., A. Freeman, and D. D. Davis. 2006. *Cognitive Therapy of Personality Disorders.* New York: Guilford Press.

Beck, J. S. 2005. *Cognitive Therapy for Challenging Problems: What to Do When the Basics Don't Work.* New York: Guilford Press.

Behary, W. T. 2006. The art of empathic confrontation: Working with the narcissistic client. *Psychotherapy Networker,* March-April, 75–81.

Bennett-Goleman, T. 2001. *Emotional Alchemy: How the Mind Can Heal the Heart.* New York: Three Rivers Press.

Campbell, W. K., and J. D. Miller (eds.). 2011. *The Handbook of Narcissism and Narcissistic Personality Disorder: Theoretical Approaches, Empirical Findings, and Treatments.* Hoboken, NJ: John Wiley and Sons. (Includes a chapter on schema therapy for narcissism by W. T. Behary and E. Dieckmann.)

Fortgang, L. B. 2002. *Living Your Best Life: Ten Strategies for Getting from Where You Are to Where You're Meant to Be.* New York: Jeremy P. Tarcher.

Fortgang, L. B. 2004. *Now What? 90 Days to a New Life Direction.* New York: Jeremy P. Tarcher.

Goleman, D. 1997. *Emotional Intelligence: Why It Can Matter More Than IQ.* New York: Bantam Books.

Gottman, J. M. 2001. *The Relationship Cure: A 5 Step Guide to Strengthening Your Marriage, Family, and Friendships.* New York: Three Rivers Press.

Layden, M. A. 2010. "Pornography and Violence: A New Look at the Research." In *The Social Costs of Pornography: A Collection of Papers.* Princeton, NJ: Witherspoon Institute.

Ogrodniczuk, J. S. (ed.). 2012. *Understanding and Treating Pathological Narcissism.* Arlington, VA: American Psychiatric Publishing. (Includes a chapter on schema-focused therapy by W. T. Behary.)

Siegel, D. J. 2001. *The Developing Mind: How Relationships and the Brain Interact to Shape Who We Are.* New York: Guilford Press.

Siegel, D. J. 2007. *The Mindful Brain: Reflection and Attunement in the Cultivation of Well-Being.* New York: W. W. Norton.

Siegel, D. J. 2010. *Mindsight: The New Science of Personal Transformation.* New York: Bantam Books.

Siegel, D. J. 2012. *The Whole-Brain Child: 12 Revolutionary Strategies to Nurture Your Child's Developing Mind.* New York: Bantam Books.

Siegel, D. J., and M. Hartzell. 2004. *Parenting from the Inside Out.* New York: Jeremy P. Tarcher.

Skeen, M. 2011. *The Critical Partner: How to End the Cycle of Criticism and Get the Love You Want.* Oakland, CA: New Harbinger Publications.

Twenge, J. M., and W. K. Campbell. 2009. *The Narcissism Epidemic: Living in the Age of Entitlement.* New York: Free Press.

Van Vreeswijk, M., J. Broerson, and M. Nadort (eds.). 2012. *The Wiley-Blackwell Handbook of Schema Therapy: Theory, Research, and Practice.* West Sussex: UK. John Wiley and Sons. (Includes a chapter on schema therapy for narcissism by W. T. Behary.)

Young, J. E. 1999. *Cognitive Therapy for Personality Disorders: A Schema-Focused Approach.* Sarasota, FL: Professional Resource Press.

Young, J. E., and J. Klosko. 1994. *Reinventing Your Life: The Breakthrough Program to End Negative Behavior...and Feel Great Again.* New York: Plume.

Young, J. E., Janet S. Klosko, and Marjorie E. Weishaar. 2006. *Schema Therapy: A Practitioner's Guide.* New York: Guilford Press.

References

Brown, N. W. 2001. *Children of the Self-Absorbed: A Grown-Up's Guide to Getting Over Narcissistic Parents*. Oakland, CA: New Harbinger Publications.

Giesen-Bloo, J., R. van Dyck, P. Spinhoven, W. van Tilburg, C. Dirksen, T. van Asselt, I. Kremers, M. Nadort, and A. Arntz. 2006. "Outpatient Psychotherapy for Borderline Personality Disorder: Randomized Trial of Schema-Focused Therapy vs. Transference-Focused Therapy." *Archives of General Psychiatry* 63(6):649–658.

Goleman, D. 2006. *Social Intelligence: The New Science of Human Relationships*. New York: Bantam.

Gottman, J., and N. Silver. 2004. *The Seven Principles for Making Marriage Work*. New York: Orion.

Hotchkiss, S. 2003. *Why Is It Always About You? The Seven Deadly Sins of Narcissism*. New York: Free Press.

Iacoboni, M. 2009. *Mirroring People: The New Science of How We Connect with Others*. New York: Farrar, Straus, and Giroux.

O'Donohue, J. 2000. *Eternal Echoes: Celtic Reflections on Our Yearning to Belong*. New York: Harper Perennial.

Scruton, R. 2010. "The Abuse of Sex." In *The Social Costs of Pornography: A Collection of Papers*. Princeton, NJ: Witherspoon Institute.

Siegel, D. J. 2001. *The Developing Mind: How Relationships and the Brain Interact to Shape Who We Are.* New York: Guilford Press.

Siegel, D. J. 2007. *The Mindful Brain: Reflection and Attunement in the Cultivation of Well-Being.* New York: W. W. Norton.

Siegel, D. J., and M. Hartzell. 2004. *Parenting from the Inside Out.* New York: Jeremy P. Tarcher.

Solomon, M. 1992. *Narcissism and Intimacy: Love and Marriage in an Age of Confusion.* New York: W. W. Norton.

Walsh, S. 2010. "20 Identifiable Traits of a Female Narcissist." June 28 blog post at *Hooking Up Smart.* http.hookingupsmart. com/2010/06/28/relationshipstrategies/20-identifiable-traits-of-a-female-narcissist. Accessed November 30, 2012.

Wordsworth, W. 1892. *The Complete Poetical Works of William Wordsworth.* New York: Thomas Y. Crowell.

Young, J. E., and J. S. Klosko. 1994. *Reinventing Your Life: The Breakthrough Program to End Negative Behavior…and Feel Great Again.* New York: Plume.

Young, J. E., J. S. Klosko, and M. E. Weishaar. 2006. *Schema Therapy: A Practitioner's Guide.* New York: Guilford Press.

Wendy T. Behary, LCSW, is founder and clinical director of the Cognitive Therapy Center of New Jersey and a faculty member at the Cognitive Therapy Center and Schema Therapy Institute of New York. She is also a distinguished founding fellow of the Academy of Cognitive Therapy. She maintains a private practice, specializing in narcissism and highconflict couples therapy.

Foreword writer **Jeffrey Young, PhD**, is the author of Schema Therapy: a Practitioner's Guide and founder/director of the Schema Therapy Institute Schema Therapy Institute of New York.

Preface writer **Daniel J. Siegel, MD**, is the author of The Mindful Brain and an associate clinical professor at the UCLA School of Medicine Center for Human Development.